A Reader's Guide to D. H. Lawrence

. . . he who wishes to see a Vision, a perfect Whole,
Must see it in its Minute Particulars, Organized . . .

Blake, *Jerusalem*: IV

'Things are so split up now. There can never be
another Shakespeare' — Lawrence, quoted by Jessie
Chambers, *D. H. Lawrence: a Personal Memoir*

'Lawrence was not Shakespeare, but he had genius,
and his genius manifests itself in an acquisitiveness
that is a miraculous quickness of insight, apprehension and understanding' — F. R. Leavis, *The
Common Pursuit*

A Reader's Guide to
D. H. Lawrence

Philip Hobsbaum

THAMES AND HUDSON

For Alisdair Gray
poet and painter

The quotations from the works of D. H. Lawrence
are by kind permission of Laurence Pollinger Ltd
and the Estate of the late Mrs Frieda Lawrence
Ravagli; William Heinemann Ltd; Alfred A. Knopf
Inc.; and Viking Penguin Inc.

© 1981 THAMES AND HUDSON LTD, LONDON

First published in the USA in 1981 by
Thames and Hudson, Inc., 500 Fifth Avenue,
New York, New York 10110

Library of Congress Catalog Card Number
80-52856

Printed and bound in Great Britain by
Richard Clay (The Chaucer Press), Ltd,
Bungay, Suffolk.

Contents

Preface

As the epigraphs to this Reader's Guide will suggest, the vision of D. H. Lawrence exists in the organization of particulars. I have chosen to consider his writing in terms of recognizable genres such as poems, stories, tales, novels, travel-books, philosophy, criticism and (in an appendix) the plays. But I have also taken chronology into account and separated the poems and stories into two periods and the novels into three. The dates in chapter headings refer to the years in which books or collections of stories were published, and the dates in the body of the text refer to probable times of writing and revision. Here it is a pleasure to acknowledge the historical scholarship of Keith Sagar and Charles L. Ross, among others who have done a great deal to clear up the vexed issue of the dating of the canon. I must also refer with gratitude to the work, as teacher as well as writer, of my old master F. R. Leavis, as well as to more recent writings, some of them unpublished, of Gāmini Salgādo, Evelyn Bertelsen, Christopher Pollnitz and B. R. Buckley. Nearer home, my thanks are due to the staff of Glasgow University Library, especially to the ever-helpful Miss Mary Sillitto; to Mrs Valerie Eden, who typed with skill and understanding various versions of this text, including the final one; to my wife, Rosemary, for all her patience and forbearance; and to my friend, the dedicatee of the book, who exemplifies in our own time the versatility and integrity which I respect so much in the life and work of D. H. Lawrence.

1 Poems (1905–19)

Love Poems (1913); *Amores* (1916); *Look! We Have Come Through!* (1917); *New Poems* (1918); *Bay* (1919)

In his earlier years, Lawrence wrote verse continuously. This work constitutes a kind of informal diary. It therefore assumes a sequential aspect. There are, between 1905 and 1919, something like ten groups of pieces. Each is clustered about a single theme. Taken in quantity they have the raw appeal of autobiography. But only a few of the items involved are articulated to the extent that they could be detached from their plasm of experience and so be termed poems.

Lawrence began, when he was a pupil-teacher in Derbyshire, with 'Campions' and 'To Guelder Roses'. 'Any young lady might have written them and been pleased with them; as I was pleased with them' (Preface to *Collected Poems*, 1928). The early influences are obvious: Tennyson's *Maud* and Rossetti's *House of Life passim* –

> The unclouded seas of bluebells have ebbed and passed
> And the pale stars of forget-me-nots have climbed to the last
> Rung of their life-ladders' fragile heights.
> Now the trees with interlocked hands and arms uplifted hold
>   back the light . . . ('Campions', 1905)

The clumsiness here is characteristic of the very early pieces. In all too many instances, the rhyme determines the sense. Yet, callow though they are, these items look forward – most immediately, to the lyrical descriptions of nature in Lawrence's first novel, *The White Peacock*, and, more remotely, to the grave, sculptured poems of Lawrence's last period: 'Red Geranium and Godly Mignonette', 'Glory of Darkness' and its final version, 'Bavarian Gentians'. Imperfectly articulated the early pieces may be, but they manifest several of the images and themes which were to concern Lawrence through his career. Many of them were written when Lawrence was studying for a teacher's diploma at Nottingham University College. His sympathy with all living things is seen in 'Dog-Tired', 'Renascence', 'Study', 'Twilight' and especially, 'The Wild Common' (*c*.1905):

> Rabbits, handfuls of brown earth, lie
> Low-rounded on the mournful grass they have bitten down
>   to the quick . . .

The psychological notation manifest in the great novels of 1915–16 is also prefigured in this remarkable piece:

> So my soul like a passionate woman turns,
> Filled with remorseful terror to the man she scorned,
>   and her love
> For myself in my own eyes' laughter burns . . .

Even so, the rhythm of the verse does little for the sense: there is too heavy a pause for an enjambement to take place after the word 'love'. The syntax, too, is functionlessly contorted. This item, like others of the period, is associated with the figure of 'Miriam', Lawrence's first love, Jessie Chambers. It survives, as the others do, mostly in terms of casual glimpses of nature imagery. Moreover, in this piece, as is true of almost all the pre-war verses, the earlier drafts are the better. In revision, even the simile of the soul as a passionate woman vanishes. It is replaced by an unfocused meditation on shadow and substance. This is the version, the version of the much-revised *Collected Poems* of 1928, that tends to be promulgated. But one can see the reasons for Lawrence's dissatisfaction. There is uncertainty here, as in all these early pieces linked with 'Miriam'. Lawrence was still in search of a theme.

Sometimes the search took the form of an exploration of roots – the young poet's local mores, the dialect of his native Derbyshire. This can give rise to intensely dramatic effects couched in dialogue which is pithy, tactile, even kinaesthetic:

> Dunna thee tell me it's his'n, mother,
> Dunna thee, dunna thee.

– Oh ay! he'll be comin' to tell thee his-sen
Wench, wunna he . . .? ('Whether or Not', c.1911)

The young man in question is engaged to the girl here, but he has also fathered a child upon his middle-aged landlady. His fiancée seeks him out 'at the railroad crossin''. However, instead of betraying remorse, the young man rounds on her: '"Hasna ter sent me whoam, when I/Was a'most burstin' mad o' my-sen. . .?"' Because she has denied him her body, his frustration has found solace in the seasoned favours of the widow with whom he lodges. The young couple, however, do get together at the end, even if a little battered by the experience – '"Kiss me then – there! – ne'er mind if I scraight – I wor fond o' thee, Sweetheart."' The past tense in that last line shows that the couple have grown up into a world no longer fresh. At his friend and editor Edward Garnett's request, according to the original Preface to the *Collected Poems*, the author altered this reconciliation into the version usually promulgated. In the revision, the young man calls down execration on both his paramours and ends his impassioned speech '"So goodbye, an' let's be"'. As with most of Lawrence's early verses, the original version is more coherent and unforced than the revised one.

This can be seen in the two main drafts of an earlier dialect piece, 'Violets' (c.1908). The scene is the funeral of a debauched young man who is truly mourned by just one of many lights-o'-love; the only one he kept secret. The description of the girl with the violets is graphic in its very irrationality and quality of unexpectedness –

'Er put 'er face
Right intil 'em and scraïghted out again,
Then after a bit 'er dropped 'em down that place,
An' I come away, because o' the teemin' rain.

The version that appears in the 1928 *Collected Poems* – the one usually reprinted – is tidier: '"But I thowt ter mysen, as that wor th'only bit/O' warmth as 'e got down theer . . ."' However, it seems, in the process of being tidied, to have lost some of its zest.

A similar point can be made with regard to others among these early ballads – the lyrical 'The Drained Cup' to a very great extent indeed:

> the moon above in a weddin' dress
> Goes fogged an' slow . . . (*c*.1911, possibly earlier)

> . . . An' ower a' the thaw an' mess
> There's a moon, full blow . . . (Revision, 1927 – early 1928)

Like many of these early pieces, 'A Collier's Wife' (*c*.1911, possibly earlier) is closely related to Lawrence's prose fiction.

> Somebody's knocking at the door
>   Mother, come down and see.
> – I's think it's nobbut a beggar,
>   Say, I'm busy . . .

> . . . 'E says, 'Tell your mother as 'er mester's
>   Got hurt i' th' pit.'
> – What – oh my sirs, 'e never says that,
>   That's niver it . . .

Lawrence seems, here and elsewhere, to be using verse as a means of finding a theme. Simple and vivid as this medium is, it looks like the raw material for the finished mode which is the prose of fine stories such as 'Odour of Chrysanthemums' and 'A Sick Collier', and the first of the important novels, *Sons and Lovers* (qq.v.). Another ballad, 'Love on the Farm' (originally 'Cruelty and Love', *c*.1907), is a draft for *The White Peacock*; see, especially, the chapter called 'The Scent of Blood'. Further, 'Red' (*c*.1911) is an early version of that novel's successor, *The Trespasser*.

There was a certain degree of wavering about, technically as well as thematically, after Lawrence took his diploma at Nottingham University College and moved to a teaching job near London. The move attenuated his connection with his roots. There are a number of doleful verses about homecomings and returns to the city – 'Last Hours' (1908), for example, and 'End of Another Home-Holiday' (*c*. 1909) –

> When shall I see the half moon sink again
> Behind the black sycamore at the end of the garden . . .?

These are pieces that belong to the Croydon period. In at least the earlier years of his sojourn there, Lawrence was most himself when seeing the town in terms of his exile from his own region. This is so in items such as 'Morning' (1909; later, 'On a Grey Morning in March'):

> . . . You tell me the lambs have come, they lie like daisies
>   white in the grass
>   Of the dark-green hills; new calves in shed; peewits
>   turn after the plough –
>   It is well for you. For me the navvies work in the
>   road where I pass
>   And I want to smite in anger the barren rock of
>   each waterless brow . . .

This poem appears to be addressed to the Miriam figure who obsessed Lawrence's youth. The same is true of other pieces of this time: 'The Almond Tree', 'Lightning' and Lawrence's first published verse, 'Dreams Old and Nascent'. But he was beginning, at last, to focus on other people.

One means of development was composition in sequences. Lawrence's landlady had a baby (Hilda Mary Jones, b.1908), and she inspired a series variously called 'Baby Songs' and 'Baby-Movements' (1909). This afforded Lawrence a fresh area of imagery – 'tiny fingers outspread', 'pale, wet butterfly', 'silk-sailed boats/Of curls'. It is true that part of the sequence was cast into a story, 'The Old Adam' (1911). Nevertheless, the sequential mode had a distinct advantage for Lawrence. It enabled him to make repeated attempts at the same theme in order to achieve a more or less definitive poem. In this case, the definitive poem is probably the 1909 version of 'A Baby Running Barefoot' that is printed in *Amores*.

> When the bare feet of the baby beat across the grass
> The little white feet nod like white flowers in the wind,
> They poise and run like ripples lapping across the water . . .

There is less syntactical blur here than in many of the earlier pieces, and the hectic run of imagery keeps pace with the high-spirited theme.

Another area of experience proved to be Lawrence's work as a teacher at the Davidson Road School, Croydon. This gave rise to a sequence of verses originally called 'The Schoolmaster'. Some of these first appeared in the *Westminster Gazette* in the summer of 1912, though they were written at intervals throughout 1909. One piece that was not reprinted, probably because it overlapped with the others, was 'Scripture Lesson':

> The hum and whisper of the class, like a little wind
> From the surf, has arisen: the boys are muttering
> The psalms . . .

Unlike the verse of the very earliest pieces, the rhythm and vocabulary here, quite delicately, act out the meaning. Another item in the sequence, 'The Best of School', was reprinted unchanged in *Love Poems*. Although it was later revised for the 1928 *Collected Poems*, its sharpest perceptions remain unaltered – for instance:

> The blinds are drawn because of the sun,
> And the boys and the room in a colourless gloom
> Of under-water float . . .

Here, again, the syntax performs a function in evoking the trance-like state of the classroom, and is reinforced in this by the internal rhymes and half-rhymes.

At least two pieces in the sequence may rank as achieved poems. Once more, the texts in *Love Poems* are the best ones:

> the faces of the boys in the brooding, yellow light
> Have shone for me like a crowded constellation of stars . . .
> ('A Snowy Day in School')

> When will the bell ring, and end this weariness?
> How long have they tugged the leash, and strained apart
> My pack of unruly hounds . . . ('Afternoon: The Last Lesson')

Partly the success lies in the admixture of narrative and commentary that helps to create the atmosphere, partly it is the kinaesthetic tendency of the vocabulary – 'tugged', 'strained' – that renders the scene concrete.

Related to these two poems is another, quite self-sufficient, which turns on the way in which the school warps the natural relationship between man and boy:

> The heads of my boys move dimly through the yellow gloom
> that stains
> The class: over them all the dark net of my discipline
> weaves . . . ('Discipline', 1909)

'Stains', 'dark net' are sufficiently concrete to evoke the scene, sufficiently moralized to act as a grim commentary upon it. All this shows that, by making several attempts at a theme, Lawrence from time to time hit off an acceptable form.

Perhaps the most notable of these early sequences is the one arising out of the illness and death of Lawrence's mother (1910–11). Never was woman more sincerely mourned. The reek of pain exhales from these poems so strongly as almost to inhibit their being read as literature. Almost they seem to be documentary: the journal of a young man's torment. The titles alone would suggest this: 'Suspense', 'Bereavement', 'Loss', 'Grief', 'The End', 'Sorrow', 'Brooding Grief', 'Submergence', 'Troth with the Dead', 'Call into Death'. Others read like appeals to a lover: 'The Bride', 'The Virgin Mother', 'The Inheritance', 'Silence', 'Listening'. Only in a few of these poems is the agony annealed into something we could call operative form; a shape which seems an inevitable expression of the meaning. This happens when Lawrence is able to harness his strength of nature imagery to act out in verse what is felt as sorrow. One would instance 'Anxiety' ('The hoar-frost crumbles in the sun') and 'At the Window' (1910), which I quote entire:

> The pine-trees bend to listen to the autumn wind as it mutters
> Something which sets the black poplars ashake with hysterical laughter;
> As slowly the house of day is closing its eastern shutters.
>
> Farther down the valley the clustered tombstones recede,
> Winding about their dimness the mist's grey cerements, after
> The street-lamps in the twilight have suddenly started to bleed.
>
> The leaves fly over the window, and utter a word as they pass
> To the face that leans from the silence, intent, with two dark-filled eyes
> That watch for ever earnestly from behind the window glass.

This, without undue explicitness, shows the dying gaze fastening on to the more forbidding aspects of a landscape, because that is all the fixity of the mind allows it to see. The clumsiness that often beset Lawrence when writing conventional, rhymed verse is here stylized into a tone at once uneasy and minatory. Even if the poem were found to predate the event it seems to commemorate, so precise is the writing that such a circumstance could hardly detract from its distinction. Unlike many items of this period, it exists in its own terms and not as part of an autobiography. Well after his mother's death, Lawrence was still writing pieces for her birthday. 'On that Day' (1911) is one example, and 'Everlasting Flowers' (1912) is another. The latter is part of the sequence, *Look! We Have Come Through!* and is set in Italy:

> The olive-trees, light as gad-flies,
>   Have all gone dark, gone black.
> And now in the dark my soul to you
>   Turns back . . .

By far the best known poem among those that group themselves around Lawrence's mother is 'Piano'. It exists in two versions, each with its own virtues. The virtues, however, are not cognate. The earlier (*c*.1906–7) begins:

> Somewhere beneath that piano's superb sleek black
> Must hide my mother's piano, little and brown, with the back
> That stood close to the wall, and the front's faded silk, both torn,
> And the keys with little hollows, that my mother's fingers had worn . . .

This places the recollection that is at the core of the poem securely in a framework, and does so with disarming authenticity. It has the charm of its details. But the stanza was dropped, and the second stanza became the famous beginning of the revised version (*c*.1911):

> Softly, in the dusk, a woman is singing to me;
> Taking me back down the vista of years, till I see
> A child sitting under the piano, in the boom of the tingling strings
> And pressing the small, poised feet of a mother who smiles as she sings . . .

This version is decidedly more polished than the earlier one. No reader would wish to lose the aural precision of 'the boom of the

tingling strings'. Nevertheless, there are qualities in the draft that
are sentimentalized in the poem. For example:

> surely the heart that is in me must belong
> To the old Sunday evenings, when darkness wandered outside . . .
> (c. 1906–7)

This avoids the tendency of the emotion to rise too near the
surface in the revision:

> the heart of me weeps to belong
> To the old Sunday evenings at home, with winter outside . . . (c. 1911)

In the earlier version Lawrence says that the child has determined
the man. In the later version, less acceptably, he says that the man
weeps to become a child. Memorable though 'Piano' is, I have
never felt it deserved the praise that Richards and Leavis accorded
it, and a glance at the unpolished but authentic draft suggests the
basis for that dissatisfaction.

All this, however, indicates how powerful were the emotions
unleashed in Lawrence by his mother's agony. They were well-nigh
uncontrollable by the technical means at his disposal. Indeed,
after her death he seems to have had a period of hyperactivity and
disturbance. Helen Corke, a fellow-teacher, testifies that, in 1911,
he became a changed man. Certainly his activities of the period
savour of mania. He abruptly broke off with Jessie Chambers,
proposed, as abruptly, to Louie Burrows, who was close to him in
his college days, and all the time used Helen Corke as a kind of
moral crutch. Many years later Corke was to comment, 'I mourned
the eclipse of those subtler perceptions which had distinguished
him earlier'.

Lawrence's output through 1911 was prodigious in quantity,
erratic in quality. It was at one with the ceaseless activity that
involved him in hectic discussions with the London *literati*, in
late-night walks, sometimes in the drenching rain; and that gave
rise to the pneumonia towards the end of the year that ended his
career in teaching. 'Miriam' had been rejected in item after item of
visual precision and bitter unease: 'Separated', 'Aware', 'A Pang
of Reminiscence' and 'A White Blossom' (1910) which I quote in
full:

> A tiny moon as white and small as a single jasmine flower
> Leans all alone above my window, on night's wintry bower,
> Liquid as lime-tree blossom, soft as brilliant water or rain
> She shines, the one white love of my youth, which all sin cannot stain.

Other pieces seem to be related, but here the same atmosphere of frustration is mingled with an almost sadistic pleasure in giving hurt: for example, 'Assuming the Burden', 'A Winter's Tale', 'Scent of Irises' ('you, your soul like a lady-smock, lost, evanescent'), 'Ballad of Another Ophelia' (*c*.1911) –

> Nothing now will ripen the bright green apples,
> Full of disappointment and of rain,
> Brackish they will taste, of tears, when the yellow dapples
> Of autumn tell the withered tale again . . .

and 'Last Words to Miriam' (1911; *Amores* version):

> Yours is the shame and sorrow,
>   But the disgrace is mine;
> Your love was dark and thorough,
> Mine was the love of the sun for a flower
>   He creates with his shine . . .

The tone of these verses is brooding and sensual. One feels the emotions are genuine, but not fully understood; stated forcefully, but, on the whole, crudely.

Strained, also, are the pieces written about this period which seem to be directed at Helen Corke. She maintained in old age that she had no physical interest in Lawrence. But Lawrence seems to have seen her as a potential lover. He reproaches her for her indifference in item after item: 'The Appeal', 'Repulsed', 'Coldness in Love', 'Excursion Train', 'Release', 'Return' (1911) –

> Does anguish of absence bequeath
> Me only aloofness when I would draw near?

and 'Lilies in the Fire' (1911):

> Ah, you stack of white lilies, all white and gold,
> I am adrift as a sunbeam, and without form
> Or having, save I light on you to warm
> Your pallor into radiance, flush your cold
> White beauty into incandescence . . .

The pieces addressed to Louie Burrows are equally hectic, but
are further characterized by an almost willed sensuality: 'Tease',
'Kisses in the Train', 'Come Spring, Come Sorrow', 'The Hands of
the Betrothed', and the best-known of them, 'Snap-dragon'
(1907):

> She laughed, she reached her hand out down to the flower
> Closing its crimson throat: my own throat in her power
> Strangled, my heart swelled up so full
> As if it would burst its wineskin in my throat,
> And choke me in my own crimson: I watched her pull
> The gorge of the gaping flower till the blood did float
>   Over my eyes and I was blind . . .

The poem was revised in 1911. Its mode of imagery melds with a
number of items that exist only in Louie Burrows's transcription.
They are English versions of translations into German from the
Arabic that were made by Lawrence's uncle by marriage, Fritz
Krenkow. As V. de Sola Pinto points out in his edition of
Lawrence's poems, these pieces relate to a sequence which
Lawrence called 'Bits' and which appear to have been written at
the end of the First World War. Here, as elsewhere, Lawrence
adopted a policy of 'waste not, want not'. In other words, what
seem to be war verses prove, in fact, to be based on pre-war
imitations of Arabic poets.

> The Prophet entered a rose garden
>   And the roses tall did shadow him
> He spread his shawl sewn with gold at the hem
>   And prayed, while the roses listened to him.
>   ('The Prophet in the Rose Garden', 1911)

> The grey nurse entered a rose garden
> Where roses' shadows dappled her.
> Her apron was brown with blood. She prayed,
> And roses wondered at her prayer. ('The Grey Nurse', c.1918)

For the rest, we have a midnight shadow drooping over a dark
divan; grey doves feeding in the fountain court; and the like.
Lawrence's reconstruction of these imagistic fragments into a
sequence – some of which was published under the title 'War

Films' – is one of the more bizarre and least noticed of his poetic ventures.

All this eclecticism shows that Lawrence had not yet found a voice. In effect, he was using verse not as structure but as plasm, to catch whatever ideas or feelings came floating through his head. Each sequence, to adopt a cinematographic metaphor, is a series of takes. Some of those sequences contain not one definitive take; others, several. The less successful sequences include those about Helen Corke and Louie Burrows; the more successful seem to me to include the poems about the Schoolmaster and those about the Mother. Even so, there are a considerable number of failures to correspondingly few successes. The concept is still that of emotional diary.

Emotional diary is, essentially, the form of *Look! We Have Come Through!* By 1912 Lawrence's life had begun to resolve itself. The plot of this sequence involves a young man eloping with a married woman; and it is autobiography. Lawrence did indeed go away with Frieda, the wife of his former language professor at Nottingham. The couple wandered between May and September 1912 through Germany, Austria and down into Italy. The pieces fall as fall the events.

> And who has seen the moon, who has not seen
> Her rise from out the chamber of the deep,
> Flushed and grand and naked . . . ('Moonrise')

> The little river twittering in the twilight,
> The wan, wondering look of the pale sky . . . ('Bei Hennef')

> A blotch of pallor stirs beneath the high
> Square picture-dusk, the window of dark sky . . . ('In the Dark')

The successful poems are those which look away from the author and his love and relate to other entities. One poem which the publishers asked Lawrence to suppress from the 1917 edition of *Look! We Have Come Through!* is a re-creation of Frieda's deserted husband, Ernest Weekley. Lawrence identifies him with a peasant eternally driving a bullock-waggon about the mountains of Tuxtal –

I stand aside on the grass to let them go,
And, Christ, again have I met his eyes, again
The brown eyes black with misery and hate, that look
Full into mine, and the torment starts again . . .

('Meeting Among the Mountains', 1912)

Lawrence did not even include this in his 1928 *Collected Poems*. Yet it is one of the most poignant pieces in *Look! We Have Come Through!* – impressive at once for its human sympathy and for its richness of descriptive detail.

Even more striking is Lawrence's most articulated poem to date, 'Giorno dei Morti' (1912). Here, for the first time, Lawrence, instead of succumbing to form, operates it. There is a structural, not a fortuitous, appositeness. The rhymes are less heavily pressed out than heretofore. This is, well before Wilfred Owen, a pararhyme varying in assonance according to the degree of emphasis required. Further, the virtual repetition of the first stanza gives the curiously enclosed effect of a sestina; highly appropriate to a static scene, representative at once of ritual and of continuity. This, together with the cadenced beat of the rhythm, eloquently enacts the chanting described in the poem. I quote this minor masterpiece in full:

Along the avenue of cypresses
All in their scarlet cloaks and surplices
Of linen go the chanting choristers,
The priests in gold and black, the villagers . . .

And all along the path to the cemetery
The round dark heads of men crowd silently,
And black-scarved faces of women-folk, wistfully
Watch at the banner of death, and the mystery.

And at the foot of a grave a father stands
With sunken head, and forgotten, folded hands;
And at the foot of a grave a mother kneels
With pale shut face, nor either hears nor feels

The coming of the chanting choristers
Between the avenue of cypresses,
The silence of the many villagers,
The candle-flames beside the surplices.

The economy of means is at one with the precision of language. This experience is not only seen but recreated and projected. It was a poet who found those precise particulars – the round dark heads of the men, the black-scarved faces of the women, the *forgotten*, folded hands of the father, the pale *shut* face of the mother. The poem is lucid without being commonplace and it is vivid without becoming hectic. Lawrence never lamented his dead mother as gracefully as he mourned this unknown son or daughter of an Italian village. There is nothing else of this order in *Look! We Have Come Through!* Other successes – 'New Year's Eve', 'Coming Awake', 'History' – have some of the casual lyricism of the early Miriam sequences, with their feeling for nature and off-beat handling of traditional metric. The failure does not come here but in the later items of the sequence, those written after 1913. Here the verse becomes more and more affected by Whitman and, seemingly in consequence, tends to diffuseness:

> To be, or not to be, is still the question.
> This ache for being is the ultimate hunger.
> And for myself, I can say 'almost, almost, oh, very nearly.'
> Yet something remains . . . ('Manifesto', 1916)

Lawrence was to mock at this kind of writing in Whitman. Yet again and again he uncritically fell into it himself. It is as though he never realized that, behind the apparent discursiveness of Whitman, lies a patterned association of ideas linking up the various strophes. Truly, Lawrence took a decisive step when he left behind the verse which was that of Hardy and which was to become that of Owen and of Edward Thomas for the dispersed cadences of Whitman which no Englishman, even to this day, has imitated altogether successfully.

Many failures were to lie ahead. There are a number of War Poems, as interesting or as fugitive as the townscapes he had sent home with letters to 'Miriam' waiting for him in Eastwood – 'Noise of Battle' (late 1914–15), and 'Bombardment' (1916–17).

> The Town has opened to the sun.
> Like a flat red lily with a million petals
> She unfolds, she comes undone . . .

There are also some haunting elegiac poems that tenuously relate to *Look! We Have Come Through!* as well as to the War – 'The Turning Back', a shorter version of this called 'Erinnyes', 'Resurrection of the Flesh', 'Eloi, Eloi, Sabachthani', 'Resurrection', all written about 1915–16. The best of these is the first, 'The Turning Back'; until recently known only in a truncated version:

> We have gone too far, oh very much too far!
> Only attend to the noiseless multitudes
> Of ghosts that throng about our muffled hearts . . .

– haunting, indeed, but tenuous. These were the years of *The Rainbow* and *Women in Love*, the great novels into which went the deepest poetic impulse of which Lawrence was capable. He was not to speak again with real effect in verse until the earliest of the *Birds, Beasts and Flowers* – 'Mosquito', written in Sicily in May, 1920.

2 Stories (1907–19)

The Prussian Officer (1914); *England, my England* (1922); *Love Among the Haystacks* (1930); *A Modern Lover* (1934)

Lawrence wrote stories throughout his working life. His shorter fiction is the backbone of his achievement. The purpose of the present chapter is to consider Lawrence's earlier work in this form.

In the very earliest stories, the prose looks backwards to Hardy and, beyond Hardy, to George Eliot.

In the kitchen of a small farm a little woman sat cutting bread and butter. The glow of the clear, ruddy fire was on her shining cheek and white apron; but grey hair will not take the warm caress of firelight . . . ('A Prelude', 1907)

. . . The empty wagon was just passing through the gap in the hedge. From the far-off corner of the bottom field, where the sward was still striped grey with winrows, the loaded wagon launched forward to climb the hill to the stack . . . ('Love Among the Haystacks', 1908, revised 1911, 1914)

This looks back to Hardy, indeed, but the reader is intensely aware of the seeing eye, the sense of nature, and more, the keen ear for language. 'Loaded', 'launched' – the alliteration gives movement to these telling words; the day is bitten to the core. Already Lawrence is more of a poet in prose than in verse.

Through the gloom of evening, and the flare of torches of the night before the fair, through the still fogs of the succeeding dawn came paddling the weary geese, lifting their poor feet that had been dipped in tar for shoes, and trailing them along the cobble-stones into the town. Last of all, in the afternoon, a country girl drove in her dozen birds, disconsolate because she was so late. She was a heavily built girl, fair, with regular features, and yet unprepossessing. She needed chiselling down, her contours were brutal. Perhaps it was weariness that hung her eyelids a little lower than was pleasant. When she spoke to her clumsily lagging birds it was in a snarling nasal tone. One of the silly things sat down in the gutter and refused to move . . . ('Goose Fair', 1909)

If setting a scene before the reader's eye is the work of an author, Lawrence has here mastered his craft. Whoever reads this would surely want to read on. In fact, however, the story as a whole is disappointing. The brilliant evocation of the goose girl and her charges – this is incidental. At the centre are two conventional lovers, and their dialogue is not up to the initial description. Unevenness of this kind is not exceptional among the earlier works of great masters; and in this Lawrence is no exception. The 'historical' 'Fragment of Stained Glass' (1907, rev. 1911) is a virtual write-off; so is the minatory 'Shadow in the Rose Garden' (1908, rev. 1913, 1914) – 'The morning was shattered, the spell vanished away'. Yet, even at this period, Lawrence was capable of distinguished achievement.

Insufficient critical attention has been paid, even now, to 'The White Stocking', yet it seems to me a masterpiece in a naturalistic mode. The story is based on an anecdote told by Lawrence's mother. Once, at a dance, she had taken out a handkerchief and had discovered, to her embarrassment, that it was really a white stocking. In Lawrence's story, the stocking is picked up by the young girl's raffish employer and treated as though it were a gage. The girl leaves his employment and marries a steady young fellow, but on two succeeding Valentine's Days her former employer sends her, along with a white stocking, a valuable piece of jewellery. She eventually lets the secret out to her husband in a mistaken attempt to tease him.

'Tease' is perhaps the best word for the coquettish Elsie. The young Lawrence with great precision shows that the impulse is basically an aggressive one. The girl is fetching, tantalizing and irrepressible. A whole series of images is evoked to suggest this – she 'ripped off a torn string of lace', 'the pearl ear-rings dangled under her rosy, small ears', 'the loose bunches of curls on either side her face danced prettily', 'she picked up her skirts to her knees, and twisted round, looking at her pretty legs in the neat stockings'. All the imagery associated with Elsie is light, balletic; she is a creature of dance.

Undoubtedly, she is to some extent aroused by her employer, Sam Adams. He, too, has a line of imagery. It is animal, sensual: our attention is drawn to his mouth – the red laugh on his face, the warm dark opening behind his whiskers. Like Elsie, he is a dancer and draws her in by his movement and rhythm. But she is not carried away by him. The showiness and assurance of the roué leave part of her untouched.

It is rather her husband on whom she depends. He is depicted in terms of firmness, hardness, reliability. 'He was the permanent basis from which she took these giddy little flights into nowhere.' But his rock-like steadiness precludes his active partnership in the dance.

The husband is what he is, and Elsie is what she is. It is their asset and their tragedy. She cannot help flirting with the likes of Sam Adams and her husband cannot help resenting it. The story ends on a note indicative of the difficulties that may be expected to beset their future years.

She sobbed aloud: 'I never meant – '
'My love – my little love – ' he cried, in anguish of spirit, holding her in his arms.

The story (1907) basically belongs to Lawrence's Nottingham period, though it was revised in 1910–11 and again, for publication, in 1914. The stories after this, like the poems of the Croydon period, show a certain tension. 'A Modern Lover' (1909) tells of Lawrence's break with Jessie Chambers. It is a self-regarding piece of work which relates to the considerably preferable story, 'The Shades of Spring' (1911, rev. 1912, 1913, and see, in *The White Peacock*, 'The Scarp Slope') – 'You wanted me to rise in the world. And all the time you were sending me away from you – every new success of mine put a separation between us, and more for you than for me . . .' But Croydon also provided Lawrence with positive experience. The instinctive sympathy with children that informed his 'Schoolmaster' sequence of poems comes up in the school stories, 'Lessford's Rabbits' and 'A Lesson on a Tortoise' (both 1908). Both are good; the latter is a little masterpiece:

'Is he alive? – Look, his head's coming out! He'll bite you? – He *won't*!' – with much scorn – 'Please Sir, do tortoises bite . . . ?' I set them sketching, but in their pleasure at the novelty they could not be still . . . 'Please Sir, has he only got four toes . . . ? Please Sir, he's moving – Please Sir . . . !'

This is the young Lawrence making use of every piece of experience he could acquire, using his quick ear and ready observation to project – in this instance – the natural curiosity of the youngsters about the alien creature who is also a real presence in the story – 'Stretching slowly his skinny neck . . . dropping his head meditatively . . .' Yet neither this story, nor 'Lessford's Rabbits' which has similar qualities, was published until 1968!

Both stories draw upon the London squalor which impinged upon the young man from the provinces. And in 'A Fly in the Ointment' (1910, rev. 1913) a girl's present of some mauve primroses sent from 'Strelley Mill' is seen as a country vision incongruously tincturing that London life; in this story, represented by a narrow, pinched-looking larcenist. Some joyless flirtation makes up the subject-matter of another of these Croydon stories, 'The Witch à la Mode' (1911, rev. 1913). But Lawrence could still see a positive: the sequence of poems about his landlady's baby is done into prose in 'The Old Adam' (1911) – 'she reminded him of a field-mouse which plays alone in the corn, for sheer joy'.

However, the stories of Lawrence in this early period that have been most influential as a group are directly concerned with experience nearer his roots; with the colliers of Derbyshire and Nottinghamshire. These stories relate in subject-matter to *Sons and Lovers*, but the scale of that work requires it to be dealt with in the next chapter. In these stories, as in that novel, almost for the first time in English, the inarticulate are allowed to speak.

Much of this achievement is due to the flexibility and precision of Lawrence's matchless prose. 'Odour of Chrysanthemums' (1909, rev. 1911) was the story that convinced Ford Madox Hueffer, the editor of *The English Review*, that he had found a genius. Its onomatopoeic beginning has been justly acclaimed:

The small locomotive engine, Number 4, came clanking, stumbling down from Selston with seven full waggons. It appeared round the corner with loud threats of speed, but the colt that it startled from among the gorse, which still flickered indistinctly in the raw afternoon, outdistanced it at a canter . . .

But this could be paralleled by extracts from any of a dozen stories of the period 1907–14. What commands respect in 'Odour of Chrysanthemums' is the degree to which the linguistic precision is sustained. The story really is a work of art and not a succession of detachable paragraphs. Through most of the story runs the image of the chrysanthemums. The miner's wife, waiting for her husband, says to her little girl, '"It was chrysanthemums when I married him, and chrysanthemums when you were born, and the first time they ever brought him home drunk, he'd got brown chrysanthemums in his button-hole."' Pink chrysanthemums hang beside the path, their ragged wisps torn by the miner's son. The mother pushes a sprig of chrysanthemums into her apron-band; indoors, there are vases holding still more of the flowers – 'there was a cold, deathly smell of chrysanthemums in the room'. One of the vases is knocked over and broken when at length the men bring her husband home on a stretcher. But he is not drunk. He is dead, killed in an accident in the pit. At this point the chrysanthemums recede in significance. They were there to symbolize the better qualities of the poor wretch, in life as well as death. His old mother says that he was a happy lad when he was young. This makes one feel that he grew up to be an unhappy man. His body in death is beautiful – '"clear and clean and white"', murmurs the old mother. The wife recognizes, however, that in life she had rejected him, as a body and as a person.

One doesn't want to attach too much autobiography to this. But in *Sons and Lovers* there is a woman who feels injured, and a husband who, like this dead man, is a collier called Walter, condemned for his drunkenness. In the story, more than in the novel, the man is rehabilitated. 'In fear and shame she looked at his naked body, that she had known falsely. And he was the father of her children.' It is a graphic way of showing how two people can live together and yet be as far apart as icebergs. 'They had denied each other in life. Now he had withdrawn.'

This is a story of 1909, Lawrence's Nottingham period; it was revised in 1911, when his interest was turning again to industrial themes. The colliery troubles of February 1912 awakened Lawrence's sympathy, and the works of the early part of that year form, together with the revised 'Odour of Chrysanthemums', a most influential group of stories.

The first of the stories of 1912 is 'The Miner at Home'. Bower and Gertie are an archetypal couple who appear in several related pieces. Bower is muscular and uncouth – he always has his dinner before washing himself. His wife, Gertie, is more refined – tall, pale, disaffected. The situation is fraught because Bower is about to participate in a strike. The wife says, '"This'll ma'e th' third strike as we've had sin' we've been married; an' a fat lot th' better for it you are, arena you . . . ?"' This is the clash between the woman who anticipates the immediate prospect of pinch and scrape and the man who sees the long run of industrial development. He tells his wife, '"Who does more chaunterin' than thee when it's a short wik, an' tha gets 'appen a scroddy twenty-two shillin'?"' The collier's complaint is as immediate now as when it was first set down. Lawrence's mastery of dialect brings the conflict home as no theorizing about it would do.

Bower and Gertie are essentially the couple in 'A Sick Collier', written in March 1912, a month later. The young miner has had an accident in the pit and torn his bladder –

'They let me lie, Lucy,' he was crying, 'they let me lie two mortal hours on th' sleck afore they took me outer th' stall. Th' peen, Lucy, th' peen . . .'
'Tha manna carry on in that form, lad, thy missis'll niver be able ter stan' it,' said the deputy.
'I canna 'elp it, it's th' peen, it's th' peen,' he cried again . . .

The precision with which Lawrence handles demotic speech brings out the husband's physicality. It is in sharp contrast with the wife's habitual quietness and control. Under the pressure of his pain, the young miner becomes a ferocious animal – '"It's her, it's her as does it . . . Kill her . . . ! kill her . . ."'

'A Sick Collier' is, like 'The Miner at Home', no more than a sketch. There is no conclusion; at the end of the story, as in the poem 'A Collier's Wife', we find the young woman discussing with a neighbour the possibilities of industrial compensation. Yet, in its insight into the mores and psychology of what used to be called the submerged classes, this stands as one of Lawrence's finest early ventures.

Handled in a lighter vein, but with equivalent skill, is a situation that arises in 'Her Turn' (1912); this time, between a middle-aged couple. The woman in question is the miner's second wife. Lawrence never loses grip on the essentials. A strike is declared, and the miner keeps his strike pay for himself. The wife, in retaliation, orders quantities of goods for the house. The deliveries are punctuated by dismayed comments from the miner: crockery ('"Whativer hast got theer?"'); linoleum ('"They come rolling in!"'); a mattress ('"Well, this is a corker!"'); a mangle ('"What dost reckon tha's been up to, Missis?"'). What the wife has been up to is the assertion of her personality in the marriage. She succeeds in her endeavour. The next week he hands her his half-sovereign without a word. Magnanimously she gives him a shilling of it to keep.

Related ground is covered, more poignantly, in 'Strike-Pay'. The characterization in the piece, for all its terseness, is astonishingly sharp. There is the ponderous union agent who has given up work in the pit for a more idle situation; the dandified miner who collects his strike pay in collar and cuffs; and the central figure, Ephraim Wharmby, who is enticed by his mates to walk to Nottingham and who loses his money on the way. His mates whip up a collection, but it is well short of the previous figure. A mere five and sixpence is the allowance he places on the table before his mother-in-law – with whom his wife and himself perforce have to lodge. When the wretched Ephraim has the temerity to ask for his tea, the mother-in-law launches out into inspired monologue – '"See him land home after being out on the spree for hours, and give his orders, my sirs! Oh, strike sets the men up, it does. Nothing have they to do but guzzle and gallivant up to Nottingham . . ."' Here Lawrence has caught the point at which moral indignation heightens demotic speech – through metaphor and alliteration – until it almost reaches the level of poetry. It is this aspect of his work that has had so much influence on later writers. I am thinking of Len Doherty, Alan Sillitoe, Stan Barstow, Stanley Middleton, Bill Naughton, Keith Waterhouse, Philip Callow, among others.

More ambitious than these sketches is yet another story of 1912, 'The Christening'. Here Lawrence uses for the first time *in extenso* a technique that grew with him in his later work; a technique of tonal patterning and contrast. It is an intricate form of repetition that he had already tried out in several poems but which, on the whole, does better in the form of the short story. The datum of this present story is the christening of an illegitimate baby, grandchild of an old collier. The different members of the family are compared and contrasted. Each has a characteristic line of imagery. The schoolteacher daughter, Hilda, is 'small and frail and rusty', 'very thin', her neck 'protruded painfully' – all imagery indicative of illness. The second sister, Bertha, is described in terms redolent of a knife – 'hard', 'abrupt', 'sharp', practically always on the move. The youngest daughter, Emma, the one who has the disgraceful child, is seen as an animal: heavy, brutal, rough, sulky, glowering – she finishes up striking her brother because of his gibes at her. All four children are shown to have been contained and dominated by the old miner. 'The very ruin of him was like a lodestone that held them in its control . . . They were only half-individuals.' This is what the story is really about: the christening of the baby is an occasion through which we see into the heart of an unhappy family.

The old man, the retired miner, is something of a triumph, even for Lawrence. His illness is evoked in words of some force – 'He was a large man, but he was going to pieces'; 'he went tilting toward the fire'; 'the broken, massive frame of her father'; he 'sat big and unheeding . . . his physique wrecked . . .'. What is impressive is not the suggestion of breaking up alone; Lawrence also gets across a sense of the man's past powers. The imagery bears connotations of the wreck of a massive machine. And there is a violence in his very clumsiness: he sways, he staggers, he slavers and rambles. Yet still, at the end of the story, unlike his children, he has energy and hope:

The day after the christening he staggered in at the doorway declaring, in a loud voice, with joy in life still: 'The daisies light up the earth, they clap their hands in multitudes, in praise of the morning.' And his daughters shrank, sullen.

This group of stories about miners – 'Odour of Chrysan-themums', 'The Miner at Home', 'A Sick Collier', 'Her Turn', 'Strike Pay' and 'The Christening' – impress me as being as good as anything Lawrence did in a naturalistic vein. They grow out of the very bones of his Englishness.

All but the first are among the last works Lawrence produced before leaving England for Germany. There he continued to revise the novel that was to become *Sons and Lovers*. He also wrote a related, though inferior, story called 'Delilah and Mr Bircumshaw' (1912), in which a wife makes a fool of her slow and heavy husband. Subsequently, as told in *Look! We Have Come Through!*, Lawrence and Frieda wandered down through the Austrian Alps to Northern Italy. Here he finished *Sons and Lovers*, started the first draft of *The Lost Girl* and, in March 1913, set that aside to begin what was eventually to become *The Rainbow*.

It is the European aspects of Lawrence's wandering years that are best shown in the short stories of this period. In several of them he tried to depict his relationship with Frieda. Some of these pieces are highly autobiographical and strongly dependent upon physical settings. 'Once' (1912) shows an inexperienced lover jealous of the men in his mistress's past. 'I lay wondering if I too were going into Anita's pocket, along with her purse and her perfumes and the little sweets she loved . . .' The Frieda and Lawrence figures are seen, still mocking, still squabbling, in 'A Chapel and a Hay Hut in the Mountains' (1912): ' "I – *why* did I take a damp match of a man like you . . . ! One could scratch you for ever and you wouldn't strike . . ." ' This is a prose equivalent of several poems in *Look! We Have Come Through!* And, as in that sequence, the human trials are shown against a natural backdrop – 'great peaks of snow . . . white, and fresh, and awake with joy . . .'. This purging effect of the high mountains was to be acted out in full in the great tales of the 1920s, 'The Captain's Doll' and 'St Mawr'. In a more circumscribed vein, 'New Eve and Old Adam' (1913) has a London setting. It shows the Lawrence figure

irrationally jealous when a telegram, making an appointment
addressed to a foreigner of Frieda's name, reaches her by
mistake.

Frieda's antecedents and connections had a fascination for
Lawrence. An anecdote told by Frieda's father, a former officer,
suggested 'The Mortal Coil' (1913), a story of the Prussian army. I
shall discuss this in relation to later developments of Lawrence's
fiction in my chapter on his Tales. But the aura which the Prussian
army had for Lawrence can be clearly seen in this, and in 'The
Thorn in the Flesh' (1913). In the latter story, a soldier salves a
humiliation that has been thrust upon him; he decides to desert. A
related but more important story, 'The Prussian Officer' (1913),
essentially resembles Melville's 'Billy Budd', a tale which, however, Lawrence would not have known at his time of writing. 'The
Prussian Officer' begins with the spectacle of a young soldier
marching in pain. It is not until the middle of the story that we
realize the nature of his difficulty. He has been tormented by his
captain – the Prussian officer of the story's title – who resents the
young fellow's physical zest and seeks to master it. The sadistic
assaults of the officer and the disintegration of the young man are
precisely detailed. 'The Captain's heart gave a pang, as if of
pleasure, seeing the young fellow bewildered and uncertain on his
feet, with pain.' Clearly, there is an unstated homosexual relationship; on both sides. The soldier may resent the attacks on his
dignity, as the anti-hero of 'The Thorn in the Flesh' did, but he is
very much emotionally dependent upon his officer. The story had
begun by focusing on the Captain's hand: it trembles when he
takes his coffee. The statement is repeated a third of the way
through. The repetition, of course, has the resonance of knowledge; by now we are able to see the nature of the relationship
between the two men. Indeed, the soldier avenges himself on the
Captain – this assault is also marked by the raising of a cup. 'And it
was pleasant, too, to have that chin, that hard jaw already slightly
rough with beard, in his hands.' But there is an ambiguity even in
his assault upon the Captain. And the assault – which kills the
Captain – also finishes off the soldier. He goes passive, and stays
crouched in the woods. This is well described in terms of the
course of nature flowing all about him: 'tap-tap-tap – it was the

small, quick bird rapping the tree-trunk with its beak, as if its head were a little round hammer . . .' He stays in the woods, dies of exposure and is finally laid beside his master in the mortuary. 'The Prussian Officer' is a disturbing story, not only because of the implied homosexuality, but also because of the psychological ascendancy that this affords the man in the socially superior position. This is a relationship in which the key constituent is the humiliation of one's fellow.

It could be argued that one's fellow could not be humiliated if he did not allow himself to be so. The roots of manhood were constantly explored by Lawrence, and much of what he has to say on the subject related, not to the exotic scenes where he later chose to live, but to what he saw as the effeteness of the England of his day. The more Lawrence travelled, the more he resented what he took to be a drastic and irreversible decline in his native country. In his late work, Lawrence was to be acerbically critical, and this attitude is prefigured in one of his greatest stories. It is called, ironically, after a patriotic poem by W. E. Henley, 'England, my England' (1915, rev. 1921).

In this story, the old England is symbolized by an apparently unchanging landscape – the shaggy gorse common, the garden which had been a garden for a thousand years, the timbered cottage which belonged to the England of hamlets and yeomen. It is symbolized, too, by Godfrey Marshall and his daughters – 'strong-limbed, thick-blooded people, true English, as holly-trees and hawthorn are English'. Into this family comes Egbert, who has married the daughter called Winifred. But he is made of quite a different paste; he is a born amateur. It is not that he is idle, exactly, but he has not been brought up to get to grips with anything. A good deal of this is indicated by his desultory work in the garden. For instance, he fills the slope with little terraces; but they are poorly shored up and so begin to bend and rot and break. He will not study; he has no profession; all he possesses is a little income sufficient to prevent him from starving. For the rest, he and his family – the children have begun to come – depend on the sturdy, old-English Marshall, his father-in-law, for sustenance. '"If he had done something unsuccessfully, and *lost* what money they had . . .!"' thinks Winifred. But his life is gardening and folk-song and Morris-dancing: a frequentation of old England, but only at the peripheries; a collecting of antiquities rather than a furthering of tradition.

Lawrence uses the figure of the unfortunate Egbert as a representative of what he himself despised in modern England: effeteness, dilettantism, people who are artistic without being artists. There is no doubt that these were features of Lawrence's time, as they are of ours. We cannot ignore the animus behind the story, especially if we reflect that the central character is based on a brother of E. V. Lucas, one of those belle-lettrists whose cultural adynamy played a significant role in the proscription of Lawrence's work. But the animus is subsumed in the fiction; and, as fiction, this is one of the finest portraits of the gentleman-amateur that we possess. 'He was like a cat one has about the house, which will one day disappear and leave no trace. He was like a flower in the garden, trembling in the wind of life, and then gone, leaving nothing to show.'

Egbert flowers in the shade of the Marshall family tree: the garden imagery persists throughout the story. The climactic moment occurs when, with the wanton carelessness of the dilettante, Egbert leaves a sickle lying in the grass. His eldest child, Joyce, falls on it and cuts open her leg. Egbert remains indecisive while the grandfather, Godfrey Marshall, insists upon a second medical opinion. The child's leg is saved, just about, but she becomes a cripple. Egbert's wife turns against him: there is a fine passage about her shutting the gates of her soul in his face. 'There was no need for her to go into a convent. Her will had done it.'

Egbert, in response, drifts. When the war breaks out, for want of anything to do he goes into the army. In the end he dies in battle. But there is nothing heroic about his death; it is a giving in to circumstance. 'No Winifred, no children. No world, no people. Better the agony of dissolution ahead than the nausea of the effort backwards.' This is the new England, with no will to live. The story is a precise evocation of a particular family at a distinctly seen time. More than that, it is a prophecy of times to come.

In his later work Lawrence was to set against this etiolated society various evocations of the primitive sources of life: the sun, ancient religion, the individual sex-drive that brings a man and woman together. These are seen at their finest in the great Tales of the early and middle 1920s. But there were, well before these, many other manifestations of Lawrence's English concerns.

In a number of stories with English settings, Lawrence explores issues which involve physical contact. This is contact both as recognition between characters and as allegory suggesting the way in which relationships develop. One of his *idées fixes* was the belief that the sense of touch is a concomitant of honesty and knowledge. 'The Horse Dealer's Daughter' (1916–17, rev. 1921) is, among other things, a poem of awakening. This can be indicated in terms of the descriptive values accorded to the daughter of a family that is about to break up after the death of its head, the horse dealer of the title. At first the girl is shown as sullen, impassive. Then follows a passage when we see into the girl's mind. Her emotional affinities are with her mother who died long ago. Now that the girl is on her own, she finds solace in tending her mother's grave. And, as if to join her mother, on the day the family fortunes receive their final knock she walks into the pond which lies in the hollow of the fields below the house. She is seen by a friend of her brothers who happens to be passing, a young doctor. She is rescued by him from the pond and is brought back to her house. When she comes to, she finds that the doctor has undressed her and wrapped her in blankets. For her, in her emotionally deprived condition, this is much more than an act of professional necessity, or even of compassion. Her access of consciousness becomes an awakening greater than the terms of the story would allow were they merely realistic. But this is more than a study in naturalism. For example, the description of the girl's awakening as a human being develops through images of sight, touch and speech. She looks full into the doctor's face – she, who initially has been described in terms of inscrutability and neutrality. When she realizes that it was he who undressed her, she goes to him on her knees, looking up at him with 'flaring, humble eyes of transfiguration'. The girl is awake at last, and able to express herself. Her new awareness compels him – he crosses what seems to be a gulf to meet her. This is the very poetry of touch: the literal details, transfigured through the imagery of water rising and eyes shining, to convey the intensity and the pain of new love.

Not contact, but what may be termed re-contact, is treated in a story set during wartime: 'Samson and Delilah' (1916). Here a man comes back after sixteen years of mining in America and seeks to re-establish himself with his wife. When she asks reproachfully whether he calls his desertion the action of a man, he replies, '"I didn't call it anything, as I know of . . ."' And, since he is her husband, and neither of them has found in the interim any other partner, he quietly settles himself by the fire. '"A bit of a fight for a how-de-do pleases me, that it do. But that doesn't mean as you're going to deny as you're my Missis . . ."'

Rather darker in atmosphere is another story set in wartime and written a couple of years later: 'Tickets, Please' (1918). Here a flirt is made to undergo a penance involving close physical contact. The effect is all the sharper in that the flirt is male and the incident takes place in the unequivocal setting of a tramyard in wartime. This story may be based on a traumatic experience Lawrence underwent in a factory where he worked for a time as a youth. But, if so, it is interesting that he sees the central figure of the story critically. This man, a young inspector, 'walks out' with rather than makes love to the various conductresses on his route. When a girl becomes interested in him, he shears off: 'he had no idea of becoming an all-round individual to her'. So his 'conquests' are illusory; he is a mere 'nocturnal presence'.

The exasperated conductresses eventually launch an assault upon his person and force him to make a choice among them. But the girl he chooses rejects him, and does so in terms that are significant – '"I wouldn't touch him."' The other girls also draw away. He leaves, a crushed man, but the girls enjoy no sense of victory. The experience has been traumatic, for them as well as him, and they are stupefied by it.

A similar theme forms the subject of 'The Blind Man' (1918). Here, the eponymous hero presses the fingers of his visitor upon his eye-sockets in order to know him better. But, though powerful in its way, it is crude compared with 'You Touched Me' (1919). This has something in common with the later tale, 'The Fox', in that it, too, involves two maiden ladies and a young male interloper. But the earlier story is done on a more realistic – indeed, physical – level. The atmosphere of the Pottery House is created, detail by detail, in terms of privet hedge, desolate yard, closed factory, frail elder sister, dumpy younger sister, bedridden father. Years ago, this father, a prosperous manufacturer of crockery, had adopted a charity boy, Hadrian, much younger than the daughters. He trained the boy to regard him as an uncle and the young women as his cousins. The youth, growing up, had left for Canada. But, in response to a summons from the old man in his last illness, he returns home. He has no thought of staying; however, a circumstance occurs to change his mind. The father has been moved downstairs; it is Hadrian who occupies what used to be his bedroom. By mistake the elder daughter, Matilda, goes to his room to wish her father goodnight.

'Are you asleep?' she repeated gently, as she stood at the side of the bed. And she reached her hand in the darkness to touch his forehead. Delicately, her fingers met the nose and the eyebrows, she laid her fine, delicate hand on his brow. It seemed fresh and smooth – very fresh and smooth . . .

It is Hadrian's brow. The tenderness of Matilda's hand wakes Hadrian in more senses than one. He tells the old man that he would like to marry her. And he meets her protest by claiming a right in her – '"You put your hand on me"'. Physical as the story is, the crucial scene is a simulacrum of sexual contact. As such, it sums up one of Lawrence's ideas about the role of the body. But it could not do that if it were not, verbally, precise in its working.

'Kiss him,' the dying man said.
Obediently, Matilda put forward her mouth and kissed the young husband.
'That's right! That's right!' murmured the dying man.

Lawrence deals more awkwardly with a much less matchable couple in 'Monkey Nuts' (1919). Here a landgirl chases, but fails to catch, a shy young soldier. Much earlier Lawrence had shown – what is a recurrent theme in his work – a well-educated girl opting for her social inferior. In 'Second Best' (1911) Frances is jilted by a Doctor of Chemistry and encourages the advances of a young farm labourer. The story is conducted against an English summer landscape; a trapped mole acts as a simulacrum of the young man. But this is a mere draft compared with the way in which Lawrence

handles the subject in 'Fanny and Annie' (1919). Here a kind of
justice is dispensed; similar to, but more defined than, that of
'Samson and Delilah'. Once more Lawrence uses a serial technique as a means of evoking character.

The ladies' maid, Fanny, is returning home, at last, to get
married to her first love, who has been waiting for her. She is tall,
erect, finely coloured; handsome, brilliant, sensitive. Her nose is
delicately arched; her hair, a rich brown; her eyes, a lustrous grey.
Her clothes are equally part of her persona: grey velour hat,
well-cut coat and skirt, grey gloves, bead chatelaine. All these
particulars of bearing, feature and dress make up the lady. But, in
doing this, they isolate her from the common herd. And it is now
her lot to live among them.

For against this distinguished décor is ranged the detritus
extruded from an ugly industrial town. Her arrival at the railway
station is greeted by furnace flames and sooty faces. Her trudge up
the hill towards her aunt's shop is observed by passers-by, the
cinema queue, the fellows on the corner. 'It is easy to bear up
against the unusual, but the deadly familiarity of an old stale past!'

Behind her, laden with cases, plods her faithful lover, Harry.
He is a commonplace fellow, a foundry-worker: arrived at her
aunt's, she watches him munching pork pie. And her own ladylike
ways serve her in no good stead when she visits him at his
mother's. '"I'm none as ormin' as I look,"' remarks the formidable Mrs Goodall, laying on the dialect thick for the benefit of her
future daughter-in-law. '"'E'd none ha' had thee for *my* tellin' –
tha hears."'

All this leads up to the crucial scene in chapel. Here, as
everywhere else, the imagery is bifurcated – deliberately so. One
image series evokes Fanny, distinguished from the others in the
chapel in her gauzy dress and beautiful lace hat. Against this is
ranged another series involving the weird old minister, the
inappropriate hymns, Harry tackling the solos and dropping his
aitches as he sings. And then occurs the worst of all the affronts to
Fanny's brilliant persona. A stout red-faced woman stands up in
the congregation and denounces the soloist – '"You look well,
bringing your young woman here with you, don't you? . . ."' This
is the mother of the 'Annie' of the title; and Annie is about to bear

a child. Harry's contention is that the child belongs as much to him as to any of six or seven fellows the girl has been with, in and out of the pubs.

But the odd thing is that this final assault, vituperative as it is, lessens the distance between the beautiful Fanny and her undistinguished environment. The attack under which she inwardly rages shows her vulnerable, like the common herd, to abuse and the ordinary attrition of life. In the evening, at the end of the story, there is one of those marvellous moments which in Lawrence often irradiate situations that look unredeemable. The family all prepare to troop off to chapel once more:

> 'You'll have to be getting ready, Fanny,' said Mrs Goodall.
> 'I'm not going to-night,' said Fanny abruptly. And there was a sudden halt in the family. 'I'll stop with *you* to-night, mother,' she added.
> 'Best you had, my gel,' said Mrs Goodall, flattered and assured.

When Fanny calls the common old woman 'mother', the warmth of human sympathy breaks through, and Mrs Goodall responds. Fanny has at last, after her fantastic wanderings, been accepted into the real world.

So even in this fine story, which far transcends the basic theme, the current of imagery which defines Fanny has implications of distance: *noli me tangere.*

The substratum of all this is the faith Lawrence always held in the instinctual alertness one finds in animals – an alertness lost by human beings in their involvement with human society. Thus, Lawrence's eye for nature, going back to his earliest sketches and observations, is considerably more than that. It is a way of defining a natural breathing positive that the sophistications of modern life are prone to forget. In 1919 he expressed this feeling in a number of exquisite nature pieces, only a few of which lie within our purview in this chapter. The immediately post-war 'Wintry Peacock' uses the bird to symbolize a young soldier who submits at home and flourishes when abroad. But Lawrence's eye reaches a far more distinct clarity of focus in two retrospective stories of his childhood. 'Adolf' (1919) tells of a rabbit adopted by his family. The imagery of this rabbit and his development seems to me as sharp as that of *Birds, Beasts and Flowers*, which was soon to supervene. At first the rabbit is passive – 'sitting against the bread as still as if it were a made thing . . .' But, as the rabbit becomes used to the family, it comes more and more to life – 'humping his back, sipping his milk, shaking his whiskers . . .' He increases in activity – peeps into the sugar-bowl, overturns the cream-jug, flees to the parlour. Indeed his behaviour becomes quite manic:

he would twinkle in a Buddhist meditation until suddenly, no one knew why, he would go off like an alarm clock. With a sudden bumping scuffle he would whirl out of the room, going through the doorway with his little ears flying . . . a little mad thing, flying possessed like a ball round the parlour . . .

On one of these escapades he brings down the lace curtains. The mother, a quirkily sarcastic presence throughout, thereupon insists that he go back to the woods. And the author confesses himself left with the memory of a derisive gesture; an insolent symbol as impulsive and uncontrollable as the coquettish Elsie in 'The White Stocking'.

'Adolf' was turned down for publication by Lawrence's friend, John Middleton Murry, critic and editor of *The Athenaeum*. It is possible that he objected to the final section of the story, where the author turns from fiction to didacticism. Indeed, the end does belong to another mode of writing and would perhaps have been better presented on its own as a small article. The story was brought into popular circulation, along with a charming companion-piece, 'Rex' (1919), by Keith Sagar in *The Mortal Coil*, an admirable selection from Lawrence's early stories. Both 'Adolf' and 'Rex' are retrospective pieces, evoking the childhood and the England that, by 1919, Lawrence had left for ever behind him – 'a man called Rowbotham bit off the superfluity of his tail in the Nag's Head, for a quart of best and bitter . . .'

What we have before 1919 are essentially five groups of stories. The earliest Nottingham stories, around 1907 and 1908, are romantic and at times over-written. Yet 'The White Stocking', in its revised form, shines out as a masterly treatment of human frailty in human relationships. The Croydon stories of 1908–11 are somewhat restricted in emotional range, yet even here the eye for natural detail redeems several of the pieces and produced a little masterpiece in 'A Lesson on a Tortoise'. The series of mining stories, stimulated by the strike of 1912, brought a vein of realism into English that at last showed industrial workers as serious human beings in a real setting. 'Odour of Chrysanthemums', 'A Sick Collier', 'Strike-Pay' and 'The Christening' are classics in this vein. Lawrence's continental wanderings of 1912–14 produced one great story in the agonized relationship of officer and man in 'The Prussian Officer'. His return to England in 1914 compelled him to link up the state of his country with the atmosphere of the war. The stories that bear witness at once to effete sophistication and to the need for physical contact include really great works, remarkable at once for linguistic subtlety and for psychological depth. I am thinking of 'England, my England', 'The Horse Dealer's Daughter', 'You Touched Me' and 'Fanny and Annie'. Had we no other stories by Lawrence, he would have gone down in English literature as one of its great masters. The flair and precision of this work, however, is all the more astonishing when we consider that these were also the years of Lawrence's greatest work in the novel: *Sons and Lovers, The Rainbow, Women in Love*. Like the stories, those novels developed out of somewhat callow beginnings.

3 Novels (1906–13)

The White Peacock (1911); *The Trespasser* (1912);
Sons and Lovers (1913)

The White Peacock (1906–9) is intimately bound up with Lawrence's youthful experiences and with his juvenile poems. He
began it, before his earliest attempts at the short story, in his last
year as a pupil teacher at Eastwood. It continued to be his main
task at Nottingham University College (cf. letter to Blanche
Jennings, 4 May 1908), and he took it through three successive
drafts. Jessie Chambers records that Lawrence's basic idea was to
take two couples and to develop their relationships. His immediate model was George Eliot, but the differences are as marked as
the resemblances.

Looked at as an ordinary novel, *The White Peacock* does not
make much sense. The 'two couples' impinge as attitudes rather
than as characters. Lettie is 'tall, nearly six feet in height . . . a
sable Persephone come into freedom . . .' The man in love with her
is George, a young farmer seen almost always in brutish circumstances – drowning a wounded cat, breaking the neck of a rabbit,
finally drinking himself into *delirium tremens*. The story is nar-
rated by Lettie's brother Cyril, whose general flaccidity Lawrence
himself came to dislike – 'a young fool . . . a frightful bore . . . I hate
the fellow . . .' (Letters, 17 and 30 July 1908). Yet Cyril has a
fiancée, flimsily based on Jessie Chambers, who figures strongly
only near the end when she announces her engagement to
somebody else. This is in a chapter ('The Scarp Slope') which is a
parallel to such short stories as 'A Modern Lover' and 'The Shades
of Spring' (qqv.).

Insofar as there is a plot, it deals with the reprehensible conduct
of Lettie in flirting with George while encouraging the advances of
the son of the local squire and coal-owner, whom she eventually

marries. This figure, Leslie Tennant, is the prototype of such later Lawrentian characters as Gerald Crich and Sir Clifford Chatterley. But he lacks their definition and is recognized mainly in his propensity for sprawling about and lying down – sometimes, it must be admitted, as a result of illness rather than mere debility. Still, that is not enough to make a character.

Yet, if the separate figures do not work as individuals, there nevertheless is a distinct sense of young people growing up in the excitement of ideas:

Having been much impressed by Sarah Bernhardt's 'Dame aux Camelias' and 'Adrienne Lecouvreur', Lettie . . . answered in the same mad clatter of French, speaking high and harshly . . . ('A Vendor of Visions')

As I worked with my friend through the still mornings . . . I told him what the professors had told me; of life, of sex and its origins; of Schopenhauer and William James . . . ('The Education of George')

There is a sense, too, of the young people beginning to drift apart; a sense allied to the natural objects that symbolically underpin the book:

we felt ourselves the centre of the waters and the woods that spread down the rainy valley. 'In a few years,' I said, 'we shall be almost strangers' . . . ('A New Start in Life')

Emily was the first to depart finally from the Mill. She went to a school in Nottingham, and shortly afterwards Mollie, her younger sister, went to her. In October I moved to London. Lettie and Leslie were settled in their home in Brentwood, Yorkshire. We all felt very keenly our exile from Nethermere . . . ('Puffs of Wind in the Sail')

The tree that had drooped over the brook with such delightful, romantic grace was a ridiculous thing when I came home after a year of absence in the south . . . ('Several Romances')

That alder, overlooking the brook, recurs throughout the novel. Images such as this are as much of a unifying factor as more conventional devices of plot and character might be. Even though the callowness of the book is obvious, it has a remarkable grasp of natural beauty. It is redolent of an England which, even in Lawrence's time, was poignantly in retreat from the modern world. The chapters are organized in terms of the seasons. All but

the last four form a continuous narrative of some fifteen hectic
months in the lives of a group of young adults.

Autumn set in, and the red dahlias which kept the warm light alive in
their bosoms so late into the evening died in the night, and the morning
had nothing but brown balls of rottenness to show . . . ('The Father')

Lettie was twenty-one on the day after Christmas. She woke me in the
morning with cries of dismay. There was a great fall of snow, multiplying
the cold morning light, startling the slow-footed twilight . . . ('Lettie
Comes of Age')

Across the infinite skies of March great rounded masses of cloud had
sailed stately all day, domed with a white radiance, softened with faint,
fleeting shadows . . . ('Strange New Budding')

And so on, through a summer of uncoiling ferns and grouped
bluebells, another autumn with gorgeous cherry-trees and crimson plums, another winter with the ice on Nethermere gleaming in
the moonlight, on to yet another spring. The seasons indicate,
too, the disintegration of the enthusiastic young group who disport
themselves in the pages of *The White Peacock*. In much the same
way, the 'Pagans' – the generic name Lawrence's friends of his
early years gave themselves – sported over the now legendary
landmarks of the Lawrence country: Lamb Close, Felley Mill,
Greasley Haggs, Moorgreen Reservoir – this last, the 'Nethermere' of the novel.

Only one episode looks like conventional novel-writing. It is
that which, paradoxically, at once gives the book its name and has
least to do with its fictional framework. It concerns the rough
gamekeeper, Annable, who was once a Cambridge-educated
curate. He at that time was married to a Lady Crystabel; the white
peacock of the title, and a dim simulacrum of Lettie. Now
Annable lives in squalor with a slatternly woman and a horde of
draggle-tailed children. In telling their story, Lawrence taps a vein
of realism like nothing else in the novel – 'A boy sat on the steel
fender, catching the dropping fat on a piece of bread. "One, two,
three, four, five, six drops," and he quickly bit off the tasty corner,
and resumed the task with the other hand . . .' ('The Education of
George')

This realism has no central place in *The White Peacock*. But, oddly enough, it forms part of the technique of the next novel, *The Trespasser* (1910). This was written in agonized circumstances during the last illness of Lawrence's mother and out of the upsets and miseries of his Croydon friend, Helen Corke. Miss Corke had been involved with a musician who killed himself. Her notes and conversations on the subject were utilized by Lawrence and fused with his recollections of a holiday taken with his mother on the Isle of Wight the previous year. The island forms the background to the love of a music master for a favourite pupil. But the lovers' agonies and ecstasies are somewhat overwritten, especially when it becomes apparent that their affair is never satisfactorily consummated.

That night she met his passion with love. It was not his passion she wanted, actually. But she desired that he should want *her* madly, and that he should have all – everything. It was a wonderful night to him. It restored in him the full 'will to live'. But she felt it destroyed her. Her soul seemed blasted. (Chapter 8)

The strain Lawrence himself was under at this period shows in the writing: the psychological notation, so powerful in the middle period, is barely under control here. Paradoxically, the best parts of the novel are those which have the least to do with his subsequent work and which, on the face of it, seem distinctly *voulu*. There is, for example, a telling scene when, after the holiday, Siegmund comes back to his suburban home and his disaffected wife and family:

He went towards the dining-room, where the light was, and the uneasy murmur. The clock, with its deprecating, suave chime, was striking ten. Siegmund opened the door of the room. Beatrice was sewing, and did not raise her head. Frank, a tall, thin lad of eighteen, was bent over a book. He did not look up. Vera had her fingers thrust in among her hair, and continued to read the magazine that lay on the table before her. Siegmund looked at them all. They gave no sign to show they were aware of his entry; there was only that unnatural tenseness of people who cover their agitation. He glanced round to see where he should go. (Chapter 22)

Lawrence's ability to get across such material as this in a mode not altogether congenial – the mode of Dostoyevsky, of Zola or

Bennett – must command respect. He spares us little of the detail in his description of Siegmund's suicide: the untouched pot of shaving water outside a locked bedroom door, the starveling window-cleaner who is asked to peer in through the shut bedroom window, the leather strap whose buckle is embedded in the corpse's neck. It is interesting that such circumstances were precisely those which Helen Corke, in *Neutral Ground*, her own version of the story published in 1933, chose to evade. But, in the end, this is newspaper documentary incompletely dramatized into art. The details are precise without being significant. And it is difficult for the reader to be engaged by a performance so willed as to seem unfelt.

Sons and Lovers, far more than *The Trespasser*, is the logical and welcome development out of *The White Peacock*. It is an autobiographical novel, started in the latter part of 1910 but revised and rewritten several times during the remainder of Lawrence's Croydon period, and finished, after his elopement with Frieda, in Gargnano, November 1912. Part of Lawrence's difficulty seems to have been in reconciling a sharp sense of his own life's experience with the claims of art. The result was a book which is to the twentieth century what *David Copperfield* or *The Mill on the Floss* were to the nineteenth.

The historical importance of *Sons and Lovers* cannot be exaggerated. Here the working classes are displayed in their soot and penury, not as figures of fun nor even as objects of compassion, but as human beings; and they are human beings with which generation after generation in the twentieth century has identified. Lawrence has shown an emergent class climbing out from the morass in which their ancestors were embedded. The theme is something of a modern archetype, made all the more effective by the force, in this particular embodiment, of imagery, narrative detail, dialogue, atmosphere.

The book falls into two parts. The first describes the early married years of a coal-miner and his wife, and also the youth and adolescence of their children. The miner, Morel, is illiterate, no match for his wife in self-consciousness and articulacy. She is a former pupil-teacher with aspirations towards the middle classes. The story is biased heavily in her direction. Nevertheless, the miner is a portrait of some complexity, and over and over again intimations of his former attractiveness and latent kindliness come through, almost in spite of the author. But what for the most part is shown to us is a conflict between husband and wife, terrible in its concentration and expenditure of energy. A representative example is when Morel, discouraged from the society of his wife, stops off at a local public house on his way home from the pit, and eventually arrives home tipsy and hungry.

'Is there nothing to eat in the house?' he asked, insolently, as if to a servant. In certain stages of his intoxication he affected the clipped, mincing speech of the towns. Mrs Morel hated him most in this condition.

'You know what there is in the house,' she said, so coldly it sounded impersonal.

He stood and glared at her without moving a muscle.

'I asked a civil question, and I expect a civil answer,' he said affectedly.

'And you got it,' she said, still ignoring him.

He glowered again. Then he came unsteadily forward. He leaned on the table with one hand, and with the other jerked at the table drawer to get a knife to cut bread. The drawer stuck because he pulled sideways. In a temper he dragged it, so that it flew out bodily, and spoons, forks, knives, a hundred metallic things, splashed with a clatter and a clang upon the brick floor. The baby gave a little convulsed start.

'What are you doing, clumsy, drunken fool?' the mother cried.

'Then tha should get the flamin' thing thysen. Tha should get up, like other women have to, an' wait on a man.'

'Wait on you – wait on you?' she cried. 'Yes, I see myself.'

'Yis, an' I'll learn thee tha's got to. Wait on *me*, yes, tha sh'lt wait on me –'

'Never, milord. I'd wait on a dog at the door first.'

'What – what?'

He was trying to fit in the drawer. At her last speech he turned round. His face was crimson, his eyes bloodshot. He stared at her one silent second in threat.

'P-h!' she went quickly, in contempt.

He jerked at the drawer in his excitement. It fell, cut sharply on his shin, and on the reflex he flung it at her.

One of the corners caught her brow as the shallow drawer crashed into the fireplace . . . (Chapter II – 'The Birth of Paul')

This, in its particularity, its narrative flow, its mastery of dialogue, is representative of the book. It is a language which utilizes even the limitations of colloquial speech as a means of defining character. Notice how the affected verbal register of the husband collapses under stress into his natural dialect: '"yes, tha sh'lt wait on me . . ."' Notice, too, the cutting emphases manifest in the vocabulary of the wife: '"I'd wait on a dog at the door first . . ."' Their very movements of speech take different directions. It is as though each of these characters, husband and wife though they are, was born to oppose the other.

Lawrence's apprehension of the children growing up is rendered in terms similarly acute and evocative.

They were brought exceedingly close together owing to their isolation. If a quarrel took place, the whole play was spoilt. Arthur was very touchy, and Billy Pillins – really Phillips – was worse. Then Paul had to side with Arthur, and on Paul's side went Alice, while Billy Pillins always had Emmie Limb and Eddie Dakin to back him up. Then the six would fight, hate with a fury of hatred, and flee home in terror. Paul never forgot, after one of these fierce internecine fights, seeing a big red moon lift itself up, slowly, between the waste road over the hill-top, steadily, like a great bird. And he thought of the Bible, that the moon should be turned to blood. And the next day he made haste to be friends with Billy Pillins, and then the wild, intense games went on again under the lamp-post, surrounded by so much darkness. Mrs Morel, going into her parlour, would hear the children singing away:

> 'My shoes are made of Spanish leather,
>   My socks are made of silk;
> I wear a ring on every finger,
>   I wash myself in milk.'

They sounded so perfectly absorbed in the game as their voices came out of the night, that they had the feel of wild creatures singing. It stirred the mother; and she understood when they came in at eight o'clock, ruddy, with brilliant eyes, and quick, passionate speech. (IV – 'The Young Life of Paul')

It is as though Lawrence had retained, as most of us do not, his sense of what it was like to be a child; the fluid relationships, the fluctuating alliances. He has, however, developed a sophisticated technique in transmitting that sense; the prose rhythms alone should assure us of that. Even the children's song is selected with an adult ear for beauty – '"My shoes are made of Spanish leather . . ."'

However, after Paul Morel, the Lawrence figure of the novel, grows up, *Sons and Lovers* transmutes into what is virtually a different book. The sympathy the author enlists for Mrs Morel is no longer opposed to the brutish husband. Rather it is set against an object who may seem considerably less legitimate as a focus for enmity – Paul's first love, Miriam. Such enmity makes this second part into a bad story for Mrs Morel.

The author seems bent on showing Miriam to be possessive. We feel his authorial presence behind his hero when Paul says to her, irritably, '"Can you never like things without clutching them as if you wanted to pull the heart out of them?"' The accusation may be valid; but, if it is, it applies beyond this immediate scene with Miriam. Paul's mother comments on the relationship between the young couple with what may seem undue heat: '"it is disgusting – bits of lads and girls courting"' (VII). The possessiveness evinced here is considerably more damaging, one would think, than any kindred emotion Miriam shows; yet it is not criticized. The mother is seen throughout the book in a series of images which are Oedipal in effect; and yet they are not judged as such. 'Suddenly their eyes met, and she smiled to him – a rare intimate smile, beautiful with brightness and love . . .' (V) 'He had forgotten Miriam; he only saw how his mother's hair was lifted back from her warm, broad brow . . .' (VII)

Paul himself lacks outline: he is too much a vehicle for the author's observations, a vessel for his impressions, to provide a critical viewpoint from which these manifestations of passion and response could be judged. The mother sickens, at the end, of a cancer, and Paul is shown helping to hasten her death. There may be suppressed aggression here. But it is not enough to inform the latter half of the book, which therefore tends to be confusing even in the myriad sharp particulars of presentation.

There is, however, a kind of deflection from what would otherwise be liable to seem a straight choice for Paul between his girl and his mother. About halfway through the book a third major female character is introduced in the person of Clara Dawes –

statuesque, emancipated and living apart from her husband. In what seems like self-defence, against his mother as well as Miriam, Paul starts an affair with her. This has all the sensual boldness that the Miriam relationship lacks. It would have had even more if caution, presumably on the part of Duckworth, the publishers, had not played down the physicality to be found in the manuscript. Yet there is an overall feeling that Clara has been brought in for the character Paul's convenience; that she is an agent to forward the plot rather than a necessary development of the book.

If the second half is considered, as it should be, in association with the chronicle of the early family life of the Morels which constitutes the first half, the novel seems vivid in its parts, amorphous as a whole. The earlier chapters were revised and selected from what was virtually a total recall of autobiographical events. As those chapters stand now, they read like a series of interconnected sketches. The social setting is deftly slotted into a narrative retailing the life of the family. And the manuscripts show that a great deal of fortuitous material was excised by Edward Garnett, Lawrence's editor, as well as by Lawrence himself. The eldest son, William, whose death is a poignant event in the finished book, would have been an overwhelming figure if he had been presented in the same detail as exists in the drafts. His feats at stone-throwing and cycle-racing, his ruthless instruction of his acolytes, his flaunting his fine physique in Highland dress, his many girls, their chatter and their letters – all these are adjuncts to a personality that would have bade fair to shift the young Paul from the centre of the stage. Though one may regret the relegation of William to a subordinate role, there is no doubt that the inclusion of all the material relating to him would have done much to disrupt the book.

Sons and Lovers, as it stands, is magnificent in its parts. No one would wish to be without the quarrel scenes between the disaffected husband and wife (Chapters I and II); the splendid tale of Paul collecting his father's wages or the scene of the children's games (II); the sad story of William's courtship and death (VI); Paul's walks in the country with Miriam (VII) and the painful scene of their parting (XI); the agony and the death of Mrs Morel (XIV). Further, each and every appearance of Mr Morel is a triumph of characterization and atmosphere, even though we may not always choose to accede to the author's moral judgments. Moreover, like the trench poetry of the First World War, the historical significance of *Sons and Lovers* may well influence the reader's aesthetic response. Its various themes – class mobility, the struggle for education, marital conflict, the Oedipus complex – have played an immense part in the consciousness of twentieth-century youth. It is, therefore, easy to conflate novel and case-history. Nevertheless, Lawrence was his own most sensitive critic. He was to go much further than this in shaping experience into a satisfactory work of art.

4 Novels (1913–16)

The Rainbow (1915); *Women in Love* (1920)

Lawrence's two greatest novels evolved from a single matrix called *The Sisters*. It was begun at his first Italian domicile, in Gargnano in 1913, and accompanied him via Germany back to England, where he was trapped by the war. The central figure of this work was the girl Ursula: restless, intelligent and in search of a suitable partner. In the person of the frenetic and deracinated Birkin, she was to find him. This material, however, went through a great deal of rehandling. One transitional stage was abandoned because of the need to give Ursula some experience of life before meeting Birkin. Thus Ursula's relationship with Birkin was relegated to what Lawrence at first thought of as a second volume. Later this became a separate novel. The bulk of the rewriting of this later stage was done during the war years (1916–17) which he spent, impecunious and neglected by the reading public, in a lonely part of Cornwall. The earlier stage of the work not only provided the central character with a good deal of personal antecedent but also produced a whole background of social history stretching back to well before her birth: the history of the Brangwen family, no less. This earlier part was eventually entitled *The Rainbow*.

The Rainbow and *Women in Love* represent an immense development upon the novel as defined by the work of the great nineteenth-century masters. One can, indeed, see Tolstoy conjoined with George Eliot in the narrative pattern: one pair of lovers converging as another pair diverges. Some have seen Dostoyevsky in the background, particularly in the disaffection from society which some of the individual characters display. And Hardy is certainly implicit in the close relationship between character, landscape and symbol that we find in *The Rainbow*.

Yet the final effect is different from any obvious prototype. Lawrence wrote to Edward Garnett (5 June 1914) saying, 'You mustn't look in my novel for the old stable *ego* – of the character . . . don't look for the development of the novel to follow the lines of certain characters . . .' It is true that there is, in *The Rainbow*, a massive structure of plot, readily identifiable as a family chronicle. The novel proceeds in three major phases: the life of Tom Brangwen; the marriage of his step-daughter to a Brangwen cousin, no blood relation; and the struggle of the daughter of that marriage, the Ursula already mentioned, to find her place in the world.

The first phase, after a stylized opening, seems traditional enough. Tom Brangwen is established as a substantial character – 'a thick-limbed, stiff, fair man with fresh complexion, and blue eyes staring very straight ahead . . .' His external actions, too, have a pictorial quality of definition. In Chapter I, 'How Tom Brangwen married a Polish Lady', he comes to his great decision in a characteristically straightforward way. He has seen this woman, a widow with a small daughter, in the road and at the vicarage where she is a housekeeper. He trims his beard, puts on clean clothes, gathers some daffodils:

'What's to-do?' shouted a friend who met him as he left the garden gate.
'Bit of courtin', like,' said Brangwen . . .

But there is a further dimension, beyond the structure of plot, beyond even the naturalistic presentation of character. It is as though Lawrence were trying to go inside character in order to show, behind the stable ego, the myriad fluctuations of impulse and empathy. The Polish lady, Lydia, accepts Tom, and this awakens in him what may best be called an inner response. It is represented in a form of psychological notation highly characteristic of Lawrence:

He had her in his arms, and, obliterated, was kissing her. And it was sheer, blenched agony to him, to break away from himself . . . Then, for a few seconds, he went utterly to sleep, asleep and sealed in the darkest sleep, utter, extreme oblivion.

From which he came to . . . He returned gradually, but newly created, as after a gestation, a new birth, in the womb of darkness . . . (Chapter I, 'How Tom Brangwen Married a Polish Lady')

The imagery of this psychological notation is drawn from darkness and light; from gestation and death; from violent changes, used as metaphor, in the organs of the body; from flame, flood, chaos and regeneration. In this instance, the external acceptance – a couple matched – is counterpointed by an imagery of the psyche showing the difficulties the couple have in coming to terms with each other:

And after a few days, gradually she closed again, away from him, was sheathed over, impervious to him, oblivious. Then a black, bottomless despair became real to him, he knew what he had lost . . . In misery, his heart like a heavy stone, he went about unliving . . . (II, 'They Live at the Marsh')

The imagery is that of exclusion, and it counterpoints the naturalistic narrative. For example, Tom on his wedding day accepts the hearty handshakes of his friends and, in an image caught up and developed later, he looks forward in anticipation to his own triumphal entry on the wedding night. But the subsequent months mock his hopes. Lydia lapses into a sort of sombre exclusiveness: she is seen as a millstone crushing him; he feels 'like a broken arch thrust sickeningly out from support . . .' (II). This image is the first intimation of the Rainbow symbolism which is one of the key sequences of the book. And though at times the barrier breaks and there is connexion between them again, the hour gives way to bereavement for her and toil at the mill with slaves for him. Indeed he feels a peasant, a serf, a servant; nothing to do with her at all: 'he was deposed, he was cast out'.

Yet the potentiality of renewal is still there. And indeed the couple come together again in their emotions. This is a result of a dialogue that reveals their potentiality. Lydia says,

'Why aren't you satisfied with me? – I'm not satisfied with you. Paul used to come to me and take me like a man does. You only leave me alone or take me like your cattle, quickly, to forget me again – so that you can forget me again.'

'What am I to remember about you?' said Brangwen.

'I want you to know that there is somebody there besides yourself.'
(III, 'The Childhood of Anna Lensky')

Things are easier for these good and simple people than for their descendants. There has been a separation, but their coming together again is a matter of recognition: his recognition that her apparent indifference might be uncertainty, hers that this had given rise to his sense of being excluded. Now the imagery of exclusion and oppression gives way to that of entry. 'They had passed through the doorway into the further space, where movement was so big, that it contained bonds and constraints and labours, and still was complete liberty.' This in its turn reflects upon the child. It is a return of the rainbow imagery; here, essentially, a symbol of married life.

She was no longer called upon to uphold with her childish might the broken end of the arch. Her father and her mother now met to the span of the heavens, and she, the child, was free to play in the space beneath, between. (III, 'The Childhood of Anna Lensky')

This counterpoint of external description with psychological notation develops in the second phase of the novel; that which deals with this child, Anna, in her young maturity. As a child she is seen in terms of her hair: thistledown, spun glass, wild fleece, a fleecy halo. In her later girlhood she is described in terms of flame: flashing, a blaze of light, a beam of sunshine. Her maturity, as a young mother, is expressed in terms of fecundity: a full ear of corn, a body to give suck, a storm of fecund life, violent fruitfulness. This is the bath of birth, the mindless motherhood from which the modern women later in the novel seek to be liberated. Anna's husband Will is described – again, in physical terms – as a vital animal. He is a hawk, an eagle, a cat, a leopard; a savage thing, a creature of the undergrowth; feral, predatory.

But Anna and Will do not exist only on a plane of physical description. The fluctuations in their relationship are given to us, again, in Lawrence's individual noting of the interior processes. The first mutual attraction is, indeed, presented externally in the physical form of the cleaving together of bodies; but the lovers seem to themselves to be 'swinging in big swooping oscillations, the two of them clasped together up in the darkness' (IV,

'Girlhood of Anna Brangwen'). On their own, after their marriage, they bury themselves in an *égoisme à deux* – like seeds in
darkness. The real world retreats: 'All that mattered was that he
should love her and she should love him and they should live
kindled to one another, like the Lord in two burning bushes that
were not consumed' (VI, 'Anna Victrix').

The imagery of burning is much advanced from the flame-like
description of Anna as a young girl. It flows on, an internal
process, into imagery of disaffection. After the first heat of the
honeymoon Anna is set against Will and 'he felt as if he was in a
black, violent underworld' (VI). When he seeks eventually to
approach her, the imagery of emptiness and dark is gradually
transfigured, through numbness, to flame once more:

his heart burned like a torch, with suffering. . . . He loved her till he felt
his heart and all his veins would burst and flood her with his hot, healing
blood . . . And at last she began to draw near to him, she nestled to him . . .
The flames swept him, he held her in sinews of fire . . . And her mouth,
soft and moist, received him . . . They lay still and warm and weak, like
the new-born, together . . . (VI, 'Anna Victrix')

Their rainbow, symbol of consummation, is transient: a sketched
symbol after the birth of the first child – 'A faint, gleaming
horizon, a long way off, and a rainbow like an archway, a shadow-
door with faintly-coloured coping above it . . .' (VI). They still
lapse into disaffection; for Will, the church, an aesthetic rather
than spiritual aspect, becomes a kind of false rainbow, an 'arch . . .
locked on the keystone of ecstasy' (VII, 'The Cathedral'). Anna
mocks his devotions, and the couple grow away from each other as
she becomes more and more a mother figure – 'always contained in
her trance of motherhood . . . her eyes full of a fecund gloom . . .'
(VIII, 'The Child'). There is a period when Will spends more and
more time from home and even has an abortive encounter with a
factory lass. Insofar as this married couple find each other again, it
is in terms of unheeding sensuality; quite the reverse of recognition. Will begins to approach his wife as a stranger – 'the other
half of the world, the dark half of the moon . . .' (VIII). It is, so to
speak, the Gothic form of the arch which always asserted 'the
broken desire of mankind' (VIII); as distinct from the round arch,

the form of absolute beauty (sexuality). They have given way to what Lawrence terms 'infinite sensual violence'. Unlike the first couple, Tom and Lydia, the union of Will and Anna survives on a dark, unknowing level; they have adequate links neither with each other nor with a whole society. Indeed, so sectioned off is Will's sensual life that 'it set another man in him free . . . He wanted to be unanimous with the whole of purposive mankind . . .' (VIII). It is a classic bifurcation between ego and super-ego; or, as Lawrence himself might have phrased it, between intuition and mind. As Anna has lost her own mind in motherhood, so Will extrapolates his from physical being into hyperactivity.

But their eldest daughter, Ursula, is a prefiguration of the modern woman. It is for her sake, so to speak, that the book came to be written. Her grandfather, as we have seen, became reconciled with his wife; her father and mother came to, at least, a working compromise; she alone is unable to match her body and her mind. Her narrative is full of protests at deprivation. She has her early troubles with her much-loved father:

'Why, you tiresome little monkey, can't you even come to church without pulling the place to bits . . .?'
. . . She shrank away in childish anguish and dread. What was it, what awful thing was it . . .?

'. . . Who's been tramplin' and dancin' across where I've just sowed seed . . .?'
. . . Her vulnerable little soul was flayed and trampled. *Why* were the foot-prints there? She had not wanted to make them . . . (VIII, 'The Child')

She asks her deepest childish question of a relative less painfully close to her:

'Will somebody love me, grandmother?'
'Many people love you, child. We all love you.'
'But when I am grown up, will somebody love me . . .?' (IX, 'The Marsh and the Flood')

This is parallel to the questions Ursula asks herself about her life as she grows up. As a schoolgirl: 'Why should one remember the things one read?' (XII). As a young pupil-teacher: 'What did it matter, what did it matter if their books were dirty and they did not obey?' (XIII). And as a university student: 'What was Latin? – So much dry goods of knowledge' (XV). It will be seen that Ursula asks two kinds of question: 'Will somebody love me . . .?' and 'Why should one remember . . .?' They are parallel, and they do not converge. The emotions and the intellect are set apart, one from the other. It is Lawrence's way of indicating the bifurcated nature of the modern consciousness.

Ursula herself is characterized as a lonely maid, a wandering spirit, a dusky fragment, a traveller on the face of the earth, a soul wandering in some other world. All her more external images are those of the traveller, the wanderer. However, she feels herself trapped in her love affairs with Winifred Inger and Anton Skrebensky. Here, the imagery goes inward and becomes a notation of imprisonment in which she herself acts the role of a weapon striving to get free. In the case of Miss Inger, Ursula finds her own edge dulled – 'a heavy, clogged sense of deadness began to gather upon her, from the other woman's contact . . .' (XII, 'Shame'). Heterosexual contact is, for Ursula, inherently more appealing. Her lover, Skrebensky, however, is not sufficiently a personality, in this eroded age, to impress himself on Ursula. Therefore her resistance to Skrebensky is all the more powerful.

There are two very explicit sexual encounters in each of which the man is represented as soft iron, corroding or yielding into nothingness; a heart melting in fear, a will broken. To Ursula he seems an inert burden, an entangling net of shadows. While Ursula herself, in Lawrence's psychological notation, appears bright as a steel blade, brilliant and hard and as coldly burning as salt. This is how Lawrence gets across a sense of the inner life. It is not that there is no structure of plot or external description of character; but we have, in addition, this notation of an inner area of conflict and withdrawal. Ursula's antagonism to the imprisoning male is identified with the moon, symbol of unsubjugated femininity:

She stood filled with the full moon, offering herself . . . She was cold and hard and compact of brilliance as the moon itself, and beyond him as the moonlight was beyond him . . . (XI, 'First Love')

That is the earlier of the two great scenes of sexual encounter. The later scene is one of reunion after Skrebensky's absence. But the differences between the lovers are irreconcilable:

There was a great whiteness confronting her, the moon was incandescent as a round furnace door, out of which came the high blast of moonlight, over the seaward half of the world, a dazzling, terrifying glare of white light. They shrank back for a moment into shadow, uttering a cry. He felt his chest laid bare, where the secret was heavily hidden. He felt himself fusing down to nothingness, like a bead that rapidly disappears in an incandescent flame.

'How wonderful!' cried Ursula, in low, calling tones. 'How wonderful. . . .!' (XV, 'The Bitterness of Ectasy')

This is to represent only one aspect of Ursula, however; the wild creature trapped in an unhealthy relationship. The question is, of course, how she is to find her natural mode of being. It appears not to be tenable upon social, urban terms. However, right through her phase of the book, Ursula has been keenly responsive to natural beauty. One poignant scene during her affair with Skrebensky represents her alone, looking out to sea, as though 'all the unrisen dawns were appealing to her, all her unborn soul was crying for the unrisen dawns'. When the sea is rough, she watches a wave bursting in a shock of foam against a rock – 'enveloping all in a great white beauty, to pour away again, leaving the rock emerged black and teeming. Oh, and if, when the wave burst into whiteness, it were only set free . . .' (XV).

As this indicates, the fulfilment Ursula seeks is associated with freedom and release. It has to do with the darker antecedents – pre-Christian, primitive – of the saint whose name she bears. This is seen in terms of the horses that Ursula encounters right at the end of the book when she believes herself to be pregnant. It is an extraordinary evocation:

Their great haunches were smoothed and darkened with rain. But the darkness and wetness of rain could not put out the hard, urgent massive fire that was locked within these flanks, never, never . . . Large, large seemed a bluish, incandescent flash of the hoof-iron, large as a halo of lightning round the knotted darkness of the flanks. Like circles of lightning came the flash of hoofs from out of the powerful flanks . . .

. . . Suddenly she hesitated as if seized by lightning. She seemed to fall, yet found herself faltering forward with small steps. The thunder of horses galloping down the path behind her shook her, the weight came down upon her, down, to the moment of extinction. She could not look round, so the horses thundered upon her . . . (XVI, 'The Rainbow')

This narrative description is orgiastic in its beat, sexually suggestive in its imagery. But it is also a kind of prefiguration of another, more finely natural, world; prefigured in terms of aspiration. The vision culminates in the final pages of the book: 'Soon she would have her root fixed in a new Day, her nakedness would take itself the bed of a new sky and a new air, the old, decaying, fibrous husk would be gone.' It is the idea of the seed emerging from the husk, the butterfly from the chrysalis; but the summation is a mystical one, designed to represent the extirpation of the social world of the novel:

And then, in the blowing clouds, she saw a band of faint iridescence colouring in faint colours a portion of the hill. And forgetting, startled, she looked for the hovering colour and saw a rainbow forming itself. In one place it gleamed fiercely, and, her heart anguished with hope, she sought the shadow of iris where the bow should be. Steadily the colour gathered, mysteriously, from nowhere, it took presence on itself, there was a faint, vast rainbow . . . (XVI)

The rainbow finally stands for a vision: the sweeping away of the corruption of factories and houses and the release of all the people on earth into a new life:

And the rainbow stood on the earth. She knew that the sordid people who crept hard-scaled and separate on the face of the world's corruption were living still, that the rainbow was arched in their blood and would quiver to life in their spirit, that they would cast off their horny covering of disintegration, that new, clean naked bodies would issue to a new germination, to a new growth, rising to the light and the wind and the clean rain of heaven . . . (XVI)

Notice the conditional tense. Powerful though this is, it is undoubtedly *voulu*. Lawrence in *The Rainbow* has written a chronicle indicating a progressive deterioration in human relationships; he has ended it with a triumphant promise amounting to

'These things shall be!' The guarantee of this vision is in the force and certainty of the writing. But one may feel that it is insufficiently rooted in the preceding narrative. Lawrence here very nearly takes leave of fiction for prophecy.

Nevertheless, *The Rainbow* is a splendidly ambitious novel, quite worthy to assume its place beside such Victorian masterpieces as *Wuthering Heights*, *Moby Dick*, *Little Dorrit*, *Our Mutual Friend* and *Middlemarch*. Its attitudes are predominantly critical, and yet they are interfused with descriptions of the Derbyshire countryside and intimate details of the life lived there, in such a way as to redeem the book from any charge of negativism. Moreover, it commands respect for the way in which it reconciles its traditional narrative of the passing generations with the psychological notation Lawrence evolved to indicate the inner moods and changing affinities of his central characters.

Women in Love takes this even further. It is possible in *The Rainbow* to point out certain symbols – the doorway, the church, the arch, the flood, the moon – that stand, at times, a little apart from the immediate perceptions of the characters. Such symbols in this way arrogate to themselves a kind of existence distinct from the characters; distinct, that is to say, from those who are deemed in the novel to experience them.

Now in *Women in Love* symbol and character are assimilated. There is no moon other than that seen, respectively, by Ursula and Birkin in their separate ways. In a kindred fashion, the world of snow that dominates the last three chapters of *Women in Love* causes Birkin to shudder while it elates a contrasting character, Gerald, into believing it his element.

The plot, too, is quite other than the massive chronological structure of *The Rainbow*. Instead of the Hardyesque march of the generations, we have in *Women in Love* a technique more akin to that of a group of inter-related short stories developed from the elliptical manner in which scenes and events are introduced in Lawrence's first novel, *The White Peacock*. *Women in Love* is to that extent more elusive than *The Rainbow*. What prevents it from being elliptical is that each chapter focuses securely on an event which is literal narrative but which also has symbolic overtones. In 'Diver' (Chapter IV) a man's swimming shows he inhabits a medium quite different from those who watch his performance. 'Coal-Dust' (IX) is an evocation of the industrial background of the novel. In 'Sketch-Book' (X), the destruction of some drawings shows, on the one hand, an artist's foreshortening of the world and, on the other, a pseudo-intellectual's hostility to art. So it is through the book: a particular event not only gives each chapter its atmosphere but acts as a framework for the psychological notation therein.

The basic datum of the book is a group of young people in various stages of social and amorous attachment. Ursula and her sister Gudrun are teachers attracted, respectively, to Birkin, a school inspector, and to Gerald, an industrial magnate. These young people meet in differing alignments at diverse gatherings: a wedding, a school, a water-party, a modish restaurant, a London flat, a house-party, various trips and excursions. This variety of encounter serves to touch in the lineaments of the modern world: country-house society, education, the artistic fringe associated with the figure of Halliday, the intelligentsia, politics and industry. All are unequivocally condemned. *Women in Love* satirizes and writes off almost everything that a contemporary reader of Lawrence might have been expected to approve. Against this back-cloth the central characters behave like people under stress, even under siege. With a terrible series of quarrels Birkin finishes off an affair with the effete Hermione, a kind of perpetual society hostess, and builds up a relationship with Ursula, whom he eventually marries. After a sufficiently sordid adventure in Soho – associated with the decadent Halliday and his crowd – Gerald starts on a willed and cold-blooded affair with Gudrun. Towards the end of the book the two couples go off on a joint holiday to Switzerland. It is a kind of cold purgatory: here their abilities are judged. Birkin and Ursula, their relationship realized, leave together. But Gerald and Gudrun, discordant, split up. Gudrun has found herself to be attracted by a decadent painter, Loerke, and Gerald, defeated, dies among the Alps.

In the opening chapter, 'Sisters', we find Ursula coolly assessing with Gudrun a rather bitter future. '"Oh, if I were tempted, I'd marry like a shot. I'm only tempted *not* to."' A good many of Ursula's attitudes are expressed in negatives and in questionings.

'She lived a good deal by herself, to herself, working, passing on from day to day, and always thinking, trying to lay hold on life, to grasp it in her own understanding.' (I, 'Sisters'). Her spirit, says Lawrence, was active, but active like a shoot growing steadily that has not yet come fully above the ground. Her growth, however, is considerably speeded up by her encounters with Rupert Birkin. Particularly she is awakened by his denunciations of the world in which they live.

In the early stages of their acquaintance Ursula's feelings are hidden even from herself. In the third chapter, 'Class-room', she is unexpectedly visited at school by Birkin, trailing his old flame Hermione in his wake. Ursula finds her work as a human being both explicitly and implicitly criticized, and, once alone, 'she began to cry, bitterly, bitterly weeping: but whether for misery or joy, she never knew'. In Chapter XI, 'An Island', Ursula is symbolically isolated by Birkin from the society she knows and therefore all the more formidably exposed to his preaching. She sees his priggishness but also his male attractiveness – 'it was this duality in feeling which he created in her, that made a fine hate of him quicken in her bowels'. Such subterranean imagery shows her struggling into a rapport with the man who is to be her lover. There are lets and hindrances, however. Chapter XIII, 'Mino', centres on the symbolic encounter of Birkin's aloof male cat with a humble female who strays into his garden. He cuffs her into submission, and this typifies the kind of male sovereignty that Ursula instinctively rejects. Birkin's 'Hamletising' (XVI) about the subjection of women causes her inwardly to shudder. 'It was a fight to the death between them – or to new life . . .' (XII). And yet, once Ursula recognizes that she is in love with Birkin, she cannot bear to be apart from him. 'Her passion seemed to bleed to death . . .' (XV, 'Sunday Evening'); '. . . all the world was lapsing into a grey wish-wash of nothingness . . .' (XIX, 'Moony').

The fascination which Birkin exerts over Ursula is different in kind, obviously, from the interest which he may be expected to have for the reader. Yet the characterization works. One individual trait that sets him apart from the other characters is his quality of speech. More than anyone else in the book, he exists in explicit utterance:

'I abhor humanity, I wish it was swept away. It could go, and there would be no *absolute* loss, if every human being perished to-morrow. The reality would be untouched. Nay, it would be better. The real tree of life would then be rid of the most ghastly, heavy crop of Dead Sea Fruit, the intolerable burden of myriad simulacra of people, an infinite weight of mortal lies . . . You yourself, don't you find it a beautiful clean thought, a world empty of people, just uninterrupted grass, and a hare sitting up . . .?' (XI, 'An Island')

Birkin has often been taken to be the voice of Lawrence in the novel, and at first reading the vehemence of his utterances would seem to confirm that view. Certainly there are passages elsewhere in Lawrence which, in passing, resemble much of what Birkin has to say. John Worthen has pointed out in a useful article on *Women in Love* what seems to be a close parallel: a letter to Waldo Frank (15 September 1917):

No, what I should like would be another Deluge, so long as I could sit in the ark and float to the subsidence. – To me, the thought of the earth all *grass* and trees – grass and no works-of-man *at all* – just a hare listening to the inaudible – that is Paradise . . .

But what we have to notice is that this was written towards the end of revising the final draft of *Women in Love*. So far from being raw material selected to be worked into art it is, rather, a self-quotation. And it was written at a time when Lawrence's state of mind corresponded closely with that of his despairing fictional character. He was trapped in Cornwall by the war, unable to leave because his passport had been confiscated and constantly under pressure from the authorities who seemed to be convinced that he was a spy. Like Birkin, at this point of his life Lawrence was exasperated by the rank obduracy of people. But Birkin could not have commanded the stretch, play and detachment to have written *Women in Love*. For most of the book he is what many of us might become under the stress of ill-health, depression and frustration. That is to say, he is not a whole man.

There is throughout an emphasis upon the paucity of his physical makeup. At various times he is described as thin, pale, ill-looking, gaunt, sick, frail, unsubstantial – 'he knew how near to breaking was the vessel that held his life . . .'. But the text runs on, immediately, 'He also knew how strong and durable it was' (XVI).

Here we have the Birkin paradox. Hermione, the old flame, knows only his frailness in health and body. She seeks to dominate him, and it is this dominance in females that he fears. But Ursula sees further than Hermione – 'a curious hidden richness, that came through his thinness and his pallor like another voice, conveying another knowledge of him' (III).

Birkin has the momentum of his anger; more, he has the power of his sexuality; and this, for all its trepidations and assertiveness, is positive. In this regard he compares favourably with Gerald. In Chapter XX, 'Gladiatorial', the two men have a wrestling match. Gerald is physically the bigger of the two, but this is substance, merely; concrete, noticeable, but with no inner reality. Birkin, on the other hand, possesses physical intelligence, sublimated energy; it is he who is truly pliant, the real presence. '"It surprised me," panted Gerald, "what strength you've got. Almost supernatural."' Birkin's strength comes from within, a kind of psychic force, as distinct from Gerald's essential emptiness. There is more antagonism than affection in the scene; decisively, it is Birkin's victory. For all their surface friendship, the men are deeply opposed. Indeed, there is a counterpart to this in the psychic battle between two other incompatibles, Ursula and the defeated Hermione (Chapter XXII, 'Woman to Woman').

It is the inner depth of Birkin that enables him to develop, as Gerald and Hermione cannot, and to come to terms with Ursula. In the earlier part of the novel he is pure denunciation and he takes Ursula to be pure animal. He pains her by denouncing love and by refusing to find her attractive. In Chapter XIX, 'Moony', he seeks to shatter the image of the moon reflected in a pond; he stones it. 'But at the centre, the heart of all, was still a vivid, incandescent quivering of a white moon not quite destroyed, a white body of fire writhing and striving and not even now broken open, not yet violated.' This is a graphic but also symbolic representation of Birkin's fear of the feminine principle.

Chapter XXIII, 'Excurse', is one of barely-suppressed violence in which Birkin and Ursula reach a measure of understanding. Indeed, it is the pivot on which their sector of the book turns. It begins with Birkin wondering why he bothers with life at all. 'Why not drift on in a series of accidents – like a picaresque novel?' Yet he brings Ursula several rings: sapphire, the symbol of chastity; topaz, a sun-symbol, the symbol of passionate love; opal, the symbol of fidelity. It is the opal that fits. But Birkin is still entangled with his past; specifically, with Hermione. The lovers quarrel over this, and Ursula hurls the rings into the mud. Birkin at last has to recognize Ursula as a person and not a subordinate. He has thought Hermione to be the perfect Idea and Ursula 'the perfect Womb, the bath of birth, to which all men must come'. It is a description that would do for the Anna of *The Rainbow*, but it will not fit here. Birkin's ability, to move Ursula to anger by his hostility or to love through his innate power, shows how wrong he is in supposing her to be some overwhelming mother-figure. He humbles himself and picks up the rings, those 'little tokens of the reality of beauty'. Ursula, too, makes her concession: she comes back to him, after their quarrel, holding a piece of purple-red bell-heather – a symbol of life, continuance, the active principle.

Then a hot passion of tenderness for her filled his heart. He stood up and looked into her face. It was new, and oh, so delicate in its luminous wonder and fear. He put his arms round her, and she hid her face on his shoulder.

It was peace, just simple peace, as he stood holding her quietly there on the open lane. It was peace at last. The old, detestable world of tension had passed away at last, his soul was strong and at ease . . . (XXIII, 'Excurse')

The old, denunciatory Birkin is, for the most part, dissolved. His understanding with Ursula grows as the narrative continues. By the end of the book they are a partnership. He needs her help to cope with the annihilating world, symbolized by the Alpine snow. Theirs is a superb expression of a particular form of marriage. Birkin says to Ursula, '"I couldn't bear this cold, eternal place without you . . . it would kill the quick of my life"'. They have to leave the snow, '"the unnatural light it throws on everybody, the ghastly glamour, the unnatural feelings it makes everybody have"' (XXIX, 'Continental'). And Birkin and Ursula go down into a life where they wander about on the face of the earth, travel light, and, as Birkin says, proleptically, '"look at the world beyond just this bit"' (XXVI). It may not be ideal – they reject the idea of a settled home and children – but for them it has a possibility of working.

Ursula had momentarily, on the heights of the Alps, reverted to what the old Birkin had seen in her – 'a bath of pure oblivion, a new birth, without any recollections or blemish of a past life' (XXIX). But this was an abdication of mind, a temporary aberration brought about by the glamour of the snow. The point is made clearly when the phrase is applied to Ursula's sister, Gudrun.

In external description, Gudrun is visually, almost oppressively, present. Her external trappings are insisted upon – garish coats, coloured stockings, decorated hats, and the like; but internally, as we see from Lawrence's psychological notation, she is vulnerable. The emotional flux that Gerald elicits from her is described in terms of electrical vibration; a thrill almost pleasure, almost pain; a melting suffusion, an electric life. As Ursula was mistaken by Birkin, so Gudrun, far more dangerously, is assumed by Gerald to be a mother-figure. In Chapter XXIV, 'Death and Love', Gudrun is sought out by Gerald after his father's death. 'Into her he poured all his pent-up darkness and corrosive death . . . And she, she was the great bath of life, he worshipped her . . .' It is an indignity that he is inflicting upon Gudrun. His relaxation and fulfilment do not communicate themselves to her; on the contrary, they bring about in her an exhausting super-consciousness. 'It was as if she drew a glittering rope of knowledge out of the sea of darkness, drew and drew and drew it out of the fathomless depths of the past, and still it did not come to an end . . .' (XXIV). If Gudrun is to find an equipoise, it cannot be with this man, who selfishly uses her to restore his own being.

But Gudrun is an artist of sorts, carving statuettes: small things that one can put between one's hands – odd small people, birds, tiny animals in wood and in clay. As her sister remarks, early on, '"she likes to look through the wrong end of the opera-glasses"' (III). Much of her conversation savours of a false aestheticism that Lawrence seems to have associated with the Bloomsbury Group. This comes out clearly in a discussion Gudrun has in Chapter XXIX ('Continental') with the painter Loerke. This name has connotations suggesting Loki, the Norse god who was a personi-

fication of evil and trickery; of Lawrence's acquaintance, Mark
Gertler, who was known for his paintings of machines, notably a
merry-go-round. The character may also relate to at least two
other painters whom Lawrence mentions in letters to Edward
Garnett (30 October 1912) and to Gertler himself (5 December
1916). Something in this little man accords with Gudrun: he is in
some ways like one of the little people in her sculptures. She
defends his picture of a horse in terms reminiscent of the famous
Bloomsbury doctrine adumbrated by Clive Bell, 'significant
form'.

'What do you mean by "it is a picture of a horse"? . . . You mean an idea
you have in *your* head, and which you want to see represented. There is
another idea altogether, quite another idea . . . *I* and my art, they have
nothing to do with each other. My art stands in another world, I am in this
world' (XXIX).

This shows Gudrun at home, so to speak, in a cult where form is
divorced from meaning. In her way she is as limited as Gerald. She
had entered into a complicity with Gerald in Chapter XVIII,
'Rabbit'. Her complicity with Loerke is just as partial. 'They had a
curious game with each other, Gudrun and Loerke, of infinite
suggestivity, strange and leering, as if they had some esoteric
understanding of life, that they alone were initiated into the
fearful central secrets, that the world dared not know' (XXX,
'Snowed Up').

The snows which threatened to kill the quick of Birkin's life
Ursula likewise found abhorrent – unnatural, full of a ghastly
glamour. But for Gudrun they are exalting – 'She wanted to gather
the glowing, eternal peaks to her breast, and die . . . (XXX). This
is another version of aestheticism.

But Gerald really is a creature of the snow. He is the realization
of a dream Loerke claims to have had; a dream of fear where 'the
world went cold, and snow fell everywhere, and only white
creatures, Polar bears, white foxes, and men like awful white
snow-birds, persisted in ice cruelty' (XXX). Gerald, more even
than Gudrun, is an insistent physical presence in the novel. The
external description has him from the first as 'pure as an arctic
thing' (I), a white diver in a separate element 'like a Nibelung'

(IV), a 'ray of cold sunshine' (IX), his body 'full of northern energy' (XVI). He is the super-ego of civilization: the director of industries, efficient, strong-willed – 'The white races, having the Arctic north behind them, the vast abstraction of ice and snow, would fulfil a mystery of ice-destructive knowledge, snow-abstract annihilation' (XIX).

It is as though Gerald from the first is destined for the great snow-peaks in which he seems to find sustenance. In Chapter XXIX, 'Continental', he feels himself as 'strong as winter, his hands were living metal, invincible and not to be turned aside'. He sniffs the air in elation: '"This is perfect."' He fulfils himself in ski-ing: 'he was more like some powerful, fateful sign than a man, his muscles elastic in a perfect, soaring trajectory, his body projected in pure flight, mindless, soulless, whirling along one perfect line of force.'

Yet it is significant that, when Gerald is asked for his thoughts, he replies, like a man coming awake, '"I think I had none."' This arctic ice-prince and captain of industry has no inner life at all; or, rather, what he has is expressed by Lawrence's notation as a void. In contradistinction to the external semblance of arctic gleam and cold sunshine, the inner life of Gerald comes across as 'a bubble floating in the darkness' (XVII); as 'something dead within him', 'the stress of his own emptiness' (XX); as a shrunken spirit (XXI). There is a 'hollow void of death in his soul', he is 'a man hung in chains over the edge of an abyss' and he is 'faced with the ultimate experience of his own nothingness' (XXIV). It is because of this essential emptiness, made unbearable after the death of his father, that Gerald seeks out Gudrun. Yet his relationship with her, whatever its short-term advantages, is seen essentially as condemnation to the mines of the underworld, 'living no life in the sun, but having a dreadful subterranean activity' (XXV). This is what marriage would be for Gerald. Compare this with Birkin for whom marriage to Ursula is 'his resurrection and his life' (XXVII).

Gerald is seen by Gudrun as a superhuman instrument 'with a million wheels and cogs and axles' (XXX). Gudrun's life with Gerald, had she had one, would have been that of the woman behind the future Member of Parliament, the geometer of industry, the Napoleon of peace, another Bismarck (XXIX). In the penultimate chapter, 'Snowed Up', she pictures 'the mechanical succession of day following day, day following day, *ad infinitum* . . . But oh heavens, what weariness!' Because of this essential deadness, Gerald alone of the quartet of lovers is at home in the Alps; and this is so, even though he dies there. He is no less unconscious when living than when, finally, Birkin sees him stiff as a board, curled up as if for sleep – 'Gerald! The denier! He left the heart cold, frozen, hardly able to beat . . .' (XXXI).

In this figure, pathetic for all its magnificence, Lawrence has invested his horror of industrial civilization and its concomitants: money, politics, cerebral will and power. The symbolic judgment is backed up by the realistic treatment of Gerald's case in Chapter XVII, 'The Industrial Magnate' – an impressive piece of social history. Associated with this is the reductive aestheticism of Gudrun: a critique of what Lawrence took to be the wrong form of art. Birkin leaves Gerald and Gudrun, twin props of a false civilization, among the mountains, and as he goes they seem to grow smaller and more isolated, one from the other. It freezes his heart (XXIX). And this is in contradistinction to the envy with which, in the same chapter, Gudrun sees Birkin and Ursula, almost in terms of the earlier Brangwens of *The Rainbow* – ' "How good and simple they look together," Gudrun thought jealously.'

This is how the book works itself out: through contrast between the outer life and the inner life of the characters; contrast between the internal reaction of one character with that of another to similar circumstances; contrast between the two men, between the two women, and between the pairs of lovers, separately and together. The novel charts the fluctuations that take place in the relationships when Birkin and Ursula, through all their trials, eventually converge in a spontaneity, a childish sufficiency, which Gerald and Gudrun can never approach. It is an acting out of Birkin's concept: to travel light.

The novel is predominantly critical: explicitly so through the initial didacticism of Birkin and implicitly in the presentation of Gerald, Gudrun and Loerke, together with more minor characters such as Hermione, Halliday the bohemian, and Thomas Crich, Gerald's philanthropic and misguided father. *Women in Love* stands supreme as an adverse view of the twentieth century.

The positive of the novel is harder to define. Partly, it resides in the fluctuating but ultimately wholesome relationship of Birkin and Ursula. Birkin begins by condemning the entire world but ends up by establishing his own identity in appreciating his wife. He also hopes for a friend who will be to him what Gerald, because of his emotional foreshortening, is not. But the reader may question whether this is enough. It is possible, given Lawrence's view of the twentieth century, that no positive could be adequately worked out in terms of the characters he was able to create. And, in his later novels, the individual scenes seem to lack an adequate fictional context. It is as though Lawrence had ceased to be capable of working out an extended form that could carry his ideas.

5 Novels (1913, 1920–28)

The Lost Girl (1920); *Aaron's Rod* (1922);
Kangaroo (1923); *The Boy in the Bush* (with
M. L. Skinner, 1924); *The Plumed Serpent* (1926);
Lady Chatterley's Lover (1928)

After the achievement of *The Rainbow* and *Women in Love*,
Lawrence seems to have been more restricted in his powers. The
handling of experience in his later years tends to be haphazard
when taken beyond certain formal limits. It is true that the smaller
forms – tales, stories, poems – in this period are often self-
contained. But the later novels are affected by a kind of overflow
from the non-fictional work — the philosophy and criticism – and
this overflow is not always assimilated into the form of fiction.

However, at first reading one would detect no falling off in *The
Lost Girl* (1913, 1920); at least, not in any of its individual parts. It
has every claim to be, so far as value is concerned, Lawrence's
fourth novel; his best, that is to say, after *Sons and Lovers*, *The
Rainbow* and *Women in Love*. Yet even many readings would not
establish this novel as a classic.

In spite of this, individual sections are masterly. The book
begins with an account of Manchester House – a highly fashionable emporium in a very unfashionable mining town. We have the
testimony of Lawrence's sister, Ada, that all this was based on
fact; and indeed the town, Woodhouse, is quite recognizable as
Eastwood, which was Lawrence's birthplace. Through the earlier
part of the novel, Manchester House sinks from being a high-class
store to becoming a cut-price shop. Then it proves necessary to let
part of the premises, and the rest becomes a small dress factory.
After this venture fails, a further area is cut off, and Manchester
House emerges as 'a long, long narrow shop, very dark at the
back, with a high oblong window and a door that came in at a
pinched corner' (Chapter I). The shop at last has become a

repository for oddments, and the owner, James Houghton, has come down in the world along with it.

We see him grubbing about the various baskets of assortments – 'still a gentleman, still courteous, with a charming voice he suggested the possibilities of a pad of green parrots' tail-feathers, or of a few yards of pink-pearl trimming or of old chenille fringe . . .' This matches Wells's *Kipps* or Bennett's *Old Wives' Tale* in particularity and acquaintance with the subject. It takes into account the pathos, as well as the comedy, of Manchester House and its owner's refusal to be put down.

Nothing in the book excels Chapter VI, 'Houghton's Last Endeavour'. By now the shop opens only on Friday evenings, selling the last of its bits and bobs and making little splashes in warehouse oddments. But, though the old man is frail, he still is lively in mind and spirit. So, in his now abundant spare time, he decides to launch a cinema. He finds a frame-section travelling theatre and furnishes it with pews from the old Primitive Chapel. And this is to be no ordinary cinema: its 'dithering eye-ache' is to be diversified by stage turns – conjurors, ballad-singers, five-minute farces and stand-up comedians. He even finds a manager, a Mr May – tight, tubby, 'reminding one of a consequential bird of the smaller species'. This Mr May is based upon an American confidence-trickster, Maurice Magnus, whom Lawrence had met in Florence and whom he portrayed at full length elsewhere (see Chapter 6, below). Within the limits set by the framework of *The Lost Girl*, he turns out to be a fine comic character. Here he is talking to the heroine about the projected cinema:

'Of cauce,' he said, 'the erection will be a merely temporary one. Of cauce it won't be anything to *look* at: just an old wooden travelling theatre. But *then* – all we need is to make a new start.'

'And you are going to work the film?' she asked.

'Yes,' he said with pride . . . 'And *you* are going to play the piano?' he said, perking his head on one side and looking at her archly.

'So father says,' she answered . . . (VI, 'Houghton's Last Endeavour')

Alvina Houghton, daughter of the house and the 'lost girl' of the title, accompanies the 'turns'; and those turns modulate the book into a different key. They include Miss Poppy Traherne, the human Catherine Wheel; the Baxter Brothers, who run up and down each others' backs; and the Natcha-Kee-Tawara, a Red Indian troupe whose members hail from such cis-Atlantic places as Paris, Switzerland and Italy.

This troupe, in particular, bulks largely in the central portion of the book, and it has been adversely criticized. But there is little to carp at in the humours of the fastidious Madame Rochard who controls the little company or in the quarrels of the four sturdy young men who form her troupe. Alvina, no longer in her first youth, is attracted by the Italian among them, Cicio; and circumstances operate to put her in his way. Her father dies, exhausted by this last, theatrical, endeavour; the troupe begins to break up under the stress of its internal rivalries; the First World War supervenes.

In the final section of the book, Alvina goes as Cicio's wife to live in a remote village in the hinterland of Naples which is his family home. The details of her trying to clean up this peasant household are as vivid as anything in the travel books – 'she looked at the floor. And even she, English housewife as she was, realized the futility of trying to wash it. As well try to wash the earth itself outside. It was just a piece of stone-laid earth . . .' (XV, 'The Place Called Califano'). The surrounding landscape is also brilliantly evoked in a manner foreshadowing the technique to be used in 'St Mawr' itself – 'what could be more lovely than the sunny days: pure, hot, blue days among the mountain foothills: irregular, steep little hills half wild with twiggy brown oak-trees and marshes and broom heaths, half cultivated, in a wild scattered fashion . . .' (XV). But the landscape is not linked up with the central character in the cohesive way of 'St Mawr', or of 'The Captain's Doll' either. The relationship of the newly-married couple develops, but it does so independently of Alvina's perception of the peasants, the house and the hills. In these wild environs beyond Naples, the prose and the preoccupations of *The Lost Girl* alter beyond comparison. We are far, in mode as well as matter, from the provincial eccentricities of Manchester House and its denizens.

One explanation for this is that the novel was largely written at Gargnano in 1913, hard on the heels of *Sons and Lovers*. But the manuscript was left in Germany during one of the Lawrences' visits to Frieda's family; and there it remained, trapped by the breakdown of communications during the war. By the time Lawrence finally got hold of the manuscript, he had decided to leave England for Sicily; and it was there, in 1920, that he completed a wholesale rewriting of the work. This may account for the disparities in approach, and there is no doubt that they tend to disrupt the book as a whole. Also distinct from the whole are matters involving several of the minor characters. There is the tragic portrait of Alvina's governess, a Miss Snow, deriving in part from the great original to be found in Charlotte Brontë's novel, *Villette*. There is the pompous figure of Dr Mitchell, a physician to whom Alvina becomes briefly engaged during a temporary rebound from the Natcha-Kee-Tawara. The faithful Miss Pinnegar, erstwhile manageress of Manchester House during its short life as a factory, provides a reliable *ostinato* to the action. But even her iterated '"You're a lost girl . . . you lost girl . . ."' cannot evolve a motif sufficient to hold the book together. *The Lost Girl* is not even a picaresque. It is really a group of loosely-related sketches, the best of which describe the humours of an idealistic shopkeeper in a prosaic Midland town.

One might mention in passing the unfinished novel, begun immediately after *The Lost Girl* was finished, called *Mr Noon*. Alvina Houghton plays a minor role in this. It tells of the adventures of a provincial Lothario, but it is very inferior. The impulse to present that particular form of social mores had evidently died.

From now on Lawrence was tempted to include quite ambitious tracts of subject-matter within his fictional framework. *Aaron's Rod* was originally written in London, Berkshire and Derbyshire in 1917–19 and was entirely rewritten, with the incorporation of a set of Italian experiences, in Sicily, 1920–21. The book is more ostensibly a picaresque novel than *The Lost Girl*. But here, too, disparate modes of writing urge the reader in different, and contradictory, directions.

The book begins remarkably well, with an incident based upon a decision made by Lawrence's father to leave his home and family. The incident plays a minor part in *Sons and Lovers*, but in *Aaron's*

Rod the departure is shown in considerable detail and in a more detached manner. There is, for example, a remarkable scene in which Aaron makes a brief return to his house. He sits in the garden shed observing his family going about their business:

Suddenly the door opened. His wife emerged with a pail. He stepped quietly aside, on to his side garden, among the sweet herbs. He could smell rosemary and sage and hyssop. A low wall divided his garden from his neighbour's. He put his hand on it, on its wetness, ready to drop over should his wife come forward. But she only threw the contents of her pail on the garden and retired again. She might have seen him had she looked . . . (IV, 'The Pillar of Salt')

This could be taken as an allegory showing that Aaron was not recognized in his family. It is, however, tellingly actual – that touch of the wetness of the wall envinces mood and atmosphere as well as verisimilitude. Indeed, there is more than a show of coherence in these earlier chapters of *Aaron's Rod*. Aaron wanders into an upper-middle-class family, and their decadent social mores play their role in contrasting with his working-class inarticulacy. But the people themselves, based on several of Lawrence's London acquaintances, soon take over as entities in their own right, and they push Aaron to the sidelines. There is lanky Jim Bricknell, become stupid and drunken as a reaction to his experiences in the late war; the tall and stag-like Julia, Jim's sister, disaffected from her sculptor husband and drawn by boredom to a passive young composer; there is Jim's fiancée, the beautiful and promiscuous Josephine Ford. Yet Julia, her husband and her lover fade out after Chapter VI, and Jim himself after Chapter VIII.

As this may suggest, *Aaron's Rod* is the most arbitrary of Lawrence's novels. Aaron crops up at Covent Garden; later, he is invited to a musical party in a village by the sea; eventually he decides to go to Italy. Characters are introduced from nowhere – to reminisce about the war as Captain Herbertson does, or, like Francis Dekker and Angus Guest, to provide a sidelight on the world of an effete aristocracy. Yet one would not wish to be without the more notable passages: the preparations for Christmas in Chapter I, 'The Blue Ball'; the first encounter with the

Bricknells and their set (Chapter III, 'The Lighted Tree'); the
scene already instanced, when Aaron silently revisits his family
(IV, 'The Pillar of Salt'); the riot scene in XIV ('XX Settembre');
the scene, based on an experience of Lawrence's own, when
Aaron is robbed – 'It was as if lightning ran through him at that
moment, as if a fluid electricity rushed down his limbs, through the
sluice of his knees, and cut out at his feet, leaving him standing
there almost unconscious . . .' (XVI, 'Florence'). This sharply
creates a sense of violation. Yet, like so much else in the book, it
stands as an isolated scene. There is no central focus, least of all in
the persona of Aaron himself. In Chapter XIII the author
explicitly admits that he attributes to Aaron all kinds of attitudes
which he could not possibly have held. To say this is to concede
that the character is amorphous. This is no light matter when one
reflects that Aaron is the only member of the cast who appears
throughout the book.

The 'rod' of the title is Aaron's flute; but this is used, as occasion
serves, to symbolize his art, his manhood or his individuality.
When the flute is destroyed in yet another Italian riot, there seems
no prospect for Aaron other than some kind of *Blutbrüderschaft*
with one Rawdon Lilly. This is a Lawrentian *alter ego* who appears
intermittently: posturing, assertive, loquacious. In his vicinity
most of the nonsense in the book transpires – ' "You, too, have the
need livingly to yield to a more heroic soul, to give yourself . . ." '
(XXI, 'Words'). There is a gap, tonal and technical as well as
moral, between this kind of writing and the particularity of the
better scenes. These, on the whole, come early in the book. But
Lilly, like a number of Lawrence's later characters, is too close to
the author to avail himself of the protective cover that a work of
fiction affords. He is all too likely to be accredited as the vehicle of
Lawrence's 'philosophy' in its most assertive strain of anti-
feminism and *Herrschaft* (see Chapters IX, XX and XXI *passim*).
Such writing assimilates all too closely to the various homilies
provided throughout the text by the authorial voice itself –
'Woman . . . is driven mad by the endless meal of the marriage
sacrament, poisoned by the sacred communion which was her goal
and her soul's ambition . . .' (Etc.; Chapter XIII).

It does not appear that Lawrence realized how imprecise in

itself his philosophical terminology was, nor how extraneous to the prevalent modes of his novel. A certain amount in this strain could, however, be tolerated if the fiction were dramatically cohesive enough to carry it. This, unfortunately, is not the case with *Aaron's Rod*.

The next novel, *Kangaroo*, is, unlike its predecessor, primarily concerned with the power process. It therefore accommodates quasi-philosophical discourse rather more gracefully than *Aaron's Rod* does, and is less dispersed in its interest. *Kangaroo*, also in contradistinction to *Aaron's Rod*, was written very rapidly. It dates from the June and July (1922) of Lawrence's sojourn in Australia en route from Sicily to New Mexico. It escapes the stops and starts of revision and, perhaps in consequence, its subject-matter is fairly clearly defined. Unfortunately, the subject was something Lawrence knew comparatively little about. He had, as most of us have, an interest in the processes of political power; but he had never been a student of politics. The detail and manipulation that seem to be for politicians the stuff of life eluded, or, at best, bored him. In *Kangaroo*, nevertheless, he tried to show something of the Australian political scene. Much of his material seems to have been derived from hearsay and from the files of the *Sydney Morning Herald* and *The Bulletin*. In particular, the novel may have been sparked off by his hearing and reading about the clashes between organized Labour and the 'patriots' of the Returned Soldiers' Political League in Sydney a year or so before he arrived in Australia. But, whatever its provenance, the venture fails for want of imaginative illumination. Lawrence did not sufficiently grasp the significance of his material:

'The Labour people, the reds, are always talking about a revolution, and the Conservatives are always talking about a disaster. Well, we keep ourselves fit and ready for as soon as the revolution comes – or the disaster. Then we step in, you see, and we are the revolution . . .' (V, 'Coo-ee')

Thus ex-Captain Jack Callcott, VC, deputy of the Diggers, to the writer R. L. Somers, persuading him to join the movement. Somers is yet another Lawrence *alter ego* and the focal centre of the book. The leader of the movement, the 'Kangaroo' of the title, also has some Lawrentian characteristics but is physically quite unlike – he is a heavy Jewish lawyer named Cooley – and this anchors his vision and oratory to the narrative much more than is the case with any such discourse in *Aaron's Rod*. But this does not make his vision inherently interesting. '"If a man loves life, and feels the sacredness and mystery of life, then he knows that life is full of strange and subtle and even conflicting imperatives . . ."' (VI).

All that Kangaroo accomplishes in his book is the provocation of a riot and his own consequent assassination. Even this is shown as being of slight import compared with his rejection by Lovat Somers who says, '"I don't love him – I detest him. He can die . . ."' (XVII). It is this, rather than the bullet in his pouch, that seems to put poor Kangaroo under. And Somers leaves Australia; and that is that.

The novel has, as always in Lawrence, extraneous details that are attractive, such as his evocation of Australian landscape:

There was an unspeakable beauty about the mornings, the great sun from the sea, such a big, untamed, proud sun, rising into a sky of such tender delicacy, blue, so blue, and yet so frail that even blue seems too coarse a colour to describe it, more virgin than humanity can conceive; the land inward lit up, the prettiness of many painted bungalows with tin roofs clustering up the low up-slopes of the grey-treed bush; and then rising like a wall, facing the light and still lightless, the tor face, with its high-up rim so grey, having tiny trees feathering against the most beautiful frail sky in the world . . . (V, 'Coo-ee').

But the most striking achievement – the only thing in the book which reaches classical status – is something which has little directly to do with the central narrative. It is Lawrence's account of his persecution in England during the First World War. The basic facts are well known. Lawrence settled on the coast of a remote part of Cornwall and became an object of suspicion to the police. He had, after all, a red beard, intellectual friends, a German wife and no very obvious means of support. And, in a powerful piece of autobiographical writing, he transfers these facts, or a good many of them, to Somers, who, like Lawrence, is turned out of his home and forbidden to enter that part of the country again. His passport, like that of his wife, is confiscated. Yet he still is required to attend a medical examination, under the pretext that the government wishes him to join the army:

he was shown into a high, long schoolroom, with various sections down one side – bits of screens where various doctor-fellows were performing – and opposite, a long writing table where clerks and old military buffers in uniform sat in power: the clerks dutifully scribbling, glad to be in a safe job, no doubt, the old military buffers staring about. Near this Judgement-Day table a fire was burning, and there was a bench where two naked men sat ignominiously waiting, trying to cover their nakedness a little with their jackets, but too much upset to care really . . .

The whole place is full of a mysterious jollity emanating from the buffers and the clerks. Somers reaches the final section where a young fellow gives him a series of instructions which at first seem inexplicable:

'Put your feet apart.'
He put his feet apart.
'Bend forward – further – further –'
Somers bent forward, lower, and realised that the puppy was standing aloof behind him to look into his anus. And this was the source of the wonderful jesting that went on all the time . . . (XII, 'The Nightmare')

This seems to me immediate in its presentation and convincing in its literal detail. The trespassers of this world often escape the consequences of their actions because human shame prevents their victims from publishing the circumstances of humiliation. Lawrence shows himself here, as nowhere in the rest of *Kangaroo*, a great writer. Not only does he grasp and project the particulars of the situation: he recognizes that the shame in this lies not with the victim but with his persecutors.

The more modest details, represented in Lawrence's descriptions of the Australian wilderness, are the very stuff of his other Australian novel, *The Boy in the Bush* (1923). This was a rewriting of an unpublished novel, *The House of Ellis*, by Mollie Skinner. Lawrence had met this lady, a former VAD, while staying at a guesthouse she ran with a friend in Darlington, Western Australia. He encouraged her to write a novel with a setting in Australian history, but his revisions and adaptations appear to have been extensive, and we may take the published work as a collaboration in which Lawrence was very much the senior partner.

The novel is two-fold. It reveals a family conflict based on Genesis 25 and 27, showing a real-life Esau and Jacob and their respective families in dispute about a landed inheritance. The cautious Jacob lives with his family in the ugly stone house at Wandoo; while the Reds – a rough crowd of men and youths descended from Esau, now dead – camp out in the wilds. Their squabbles and rivalries, however, form no more than a back-cloth to what must be taken as the main theme of the book. This is the maturing and development of Jack Grant, a young Englishman emigrating to the Australia of 1882. His progress is seen in stages: all vivid, all fresh. There is his attempt to ride an uncontrollable horse (Chapter 5, 'The Lambs Come Home'); his first experience of a kangaroo hunt (7, 'Out Back and Some Letters'); a marathon Hogmanay party where he takes his first woman (9, 'New Year's Eve'); his fight almost to the death with the worst of the Reds, the so-called Big Easu (11, 'Blows'); his killing of Easu and sub-sequent exposure to the wilderness – 'he tramped on, through the brown heath-like undergrowth, past the ghost-like trunks of the scattered gum-trees, over the fallen burnt-out trunks of charred trees, past the bushes of young gum-trees . . .' (21 'Lost'). The chronicle of Jack's wanderings together with Lawrence's keen eye for landscape keep *The Boy in the Bush* fresh when the philosophy and politics of more pretentious works have failed. Reviewers at the time were shocked by Jack's resolution, framed towards the end of the book, to have two wives; but they blew this up out of all proportion. It is a limitation of *The Boy in the Bush*, but not a weakness, that the motivations of the central characters are tolerated. Its foreshortening serves a narrative purpose. In no bad sense this novel deserves to be termed a fine boys' book. Certainly it incorporates such powerful archetypes as the Quest, the Fight and the Sojourn in the Wilderness.

In comparison, *The Plumed Serpent* is far more individual in its plotting. But this is an individuality not necessarily welcome. The book was first written in Mexico in the May and June of 1923 and revised in late 1924 and in 1925. It tells how two men, a scholar and a general, displace the Christian religion in Mexico and revive the cult of the ancient gods. This is apparently a means of reforming the government of the country. The whole conception makes the schemes of Kangaroo and his Diggers look like reasoned reality.

The book is seen through the eyes of an Anglo-Irish widow, Kate Leslie, who eventually marries the general. The narrative is painstakingly literal:

People were beginning to file into the church. Kate heard the strange sound of the naked feet of the men on the black, polished floor, the white figures stole forward towards the altar steps, the dark faces gazing round in wonder, men crossing themselves involuntarily. Throngs of men slowly flooded in, and women came half running, to crouch on the floor and cover their faces. Kate crouched down too . . . (XXI, 'The Opening of the Church')

But literal as this is, it is not convincing. There is a functionless clumsiness in the prose ('stole forward towards') and an imprecision of imagery ('the men slowly flooded in') that makes the book monotonous, even rebarbative. It is not helped, either, by the hymns to the serpent god, Quetzalcoatl, that intersperse the text. These hymns waver between Ossian on the one hand and Moody and Sankey on the other. And we may take exception to the manner as well as the matter of Lawrence's theory of sex-domination in *The Plumed Serpent* – 'It was the leap of the old, antediluvian blood-male into unison with her. And for this, without her knowing, her innermost blood had been thudding all the time . . .' (XXVI).

Lawrence being Lawrence, there are times when the scholarly Don Ramón and soldierly Don Cipriano, together with the attendant Kate, fade before the Mexican landscape and the vivid detail of the peasant life of the country. But this is only to say that, among the longueurs of *The Plumed Serpent*, we glimpse hints of *Mornings in Mexico* or, even better, the shadowy lineaments of the settings which so vivify 'St Mawr', 'The Princess' and 'The Woman Who Rode Away'.

It is the analysis of human society demanded by the large-scale novel that defeats Lawrence in these later stages. The very scope of the form tempted Lawrence into his weakest areas: preaching and crypto-philosophy. This is the tendency that grows in success-ive revisions of Lawrence's last, and almost his worst, novel: *Lady Chatterley's Lover*.

The first version, commonly called *The First Lady Chatterley*, was written after Lawrence's return from New Mexico, at the Villa Mirenda near Florence, in just over a month; October–November, 1926. It had been conceived as a short story and, in some ways, would have been better as one. Even in the earliest extant version there is a ballad-like lyricism that carries the narrative over some of the awkward questions that could have been raised. Here we have the basic situation: a healthy young woman married to a paralysed baronet and having an affair with his gamekeeper.

Subsequent versions overlaid this with worries about social classification; with a plethora of sexual detail; with a great deal of didacticism. In each successive draft, *John Thomas and Lady Jane* (1926–27) and *Lady Chatterley's Lover* (1927–28), Sir Clifford Chatterley becomes more objectionable and the gamekeeper more of a gentleman.

My contention is that, in each version, every change is a change for the worse. In the original version, the relationship between Sir Clifford and his gamekeeper is very much that of officer and soldier. The narrative is kept brisk and terse. The point can be made with one of the better scenes of *The First Lady Chatterley*. It is the description of Sir Clifford's mechanical wheelchair becoming stuck while he is trying to steer it up a hill.

'She's doing it all right,' said Clifford, looking round in triumph, only to see Parkin's red face over his shoulder.

'Are you pushing?'

'Ay, a bit.'

'Don't then! I asked you not.'

'Why –' Parkin began, slackening.

'Let go!' said Clifford; 'she's got to make it.'

'Ay – got to!' said the keeper.

And he released the chair: which immediately seemed to choke.

In the second version, there is a little over-elaboration which leads to mild diffuseness, and Sir Clifford's attitude is more overbearing and hostile – ' "*Let her try* –" ' commanded Clifford. "She's *got* to do it" ' (*John Thomas and Lady Jane*).

But the final version, what we now know as *Lady Chatterley's Lover*, is far more wordy and elaborate, and the elaboration serves no dramatic function. Not only is Sir Clifford even more antagonistic, but the keeper is made more frail and is shown to suffer.

'You see, she's doing it!' said Clifford, victorious, glancing over his shoulder. Then he saw the keeper's face.

'Are you pushing her?'

'She won't do it without.'

'Leave her alone. I asked you not.'

'She won't do it.'

'*Let her try!*' snarled Clifford, with all his emphasis . . . (*Lady Chatterley's Lover*, 13)

From being (wrongly) triumphant Clifford is revised into being (wrongly) victorious. From saying 'Let go' in the first version and commanding 'Let her try' in the second, he is reduced to *snarling* '*Let her try*' in the third – with all his emphasis, indeed! But it won't do. Lawrence has a story which is inherently on the side of Sir Clifford Chatterley, and all his efforts cannot make it go far in the other direction. Clifford is by no means a routine eldest son; he is no mere inheritor. He is, rather, an intellectual; severely wounded in the war, but fighting his disability. He rallies round and begins to write again. He pours his energies into his coal-mines and makes them pay. And he is deceived by his wife with his own gamekeeper.

Even the first and most simple version of this plot is assailable by doubts as to the alignment of the reader's sympathies. It is one thing to criticize the great warhorse Gerald in *Women in Love*; it is quite another to attack a paraplegic who is trying to put together the wreckage the war has made of his life. And Lawrence commits in his later drafts the error of doubling and redoubling the burden of opprobrium that Clifford has to bear. When the wheelchair finally fails, the first version of the scene has Clifford exclaiming ' "For God's sake –" ' in irritation; in the second version he cries out in anger; but in the third, ' "For God's sake!" cried Clifford in terror.' In terror! it is as though Lawrence has no stone too heavy to hurl at Sir Clifford. Bully, boor, antagonist; and now, a coward! But the greater the amount of contumely put upon Sir Clifford's shoulders, the more the hapless condition of the man fights back against the tenor of the book.

So the final version of *Lady Chatterley's Lover* seems to me quite meretricious. In the initial draft, the gamekeeper might be acceptable as a character who was the working-class son of a collier, and a ranker in the First World War. But in the third *Lady Chatterley* he is built up into a scholarship boy, a clerk whose love of horses led him to be first a blacksmith and then an officer in the cavalry, and to become after the war a gamekeeper only as a reaction to his years of middle-class life. It turns out that his lapses into dialect – in contradistinction to the earliest draft – are only sportive and that his basic speech is standard English. He even shares some of Lawrence's notions; for example, a belief that the miners could be regenerated if one dressed them in tight red trousers. Clearly the directness of the original plot is obfuscated by such elaborations. It is hard to see what advantage there is in adapting the gamekeeper into yet another Rawdon Lilly or Lovat Somers; another conduit for Lawrence's philosophy.

One may also take exception to the layers of sexual explicitness that are added to the original. All kinds of play may take place between two lovers, from wreathing flowers in each others' pubic hair to buggery – which is what I take to be the 'phallic hunting out' celebrated in Chapter 16 of *Lady Chatterley's Lover*. But narrating all this to uninvolved third parties as a pattern of behaviour complete with mythopoeic and even prophetic over-tones – that is quite another matter. The lapse of taste is not only in topic but in tone: 'She felt, now, she had come to the real bedrock of her nature, and was essentially shameless.' The manner of endorsement seems shrill. This is the mode of Ursula's horses in *The Rainbow* gone decidedly wrong.

Certainly it does nothing for Connie Chatterley herself as a character. She lacks definition: she is merely a body to be excited, a set of loins to be hunted out. 'That was how it was! That was life! That was how oneself really was!' (16). The assertion leaves us puzzled as to why Lawrence has chosen to put his readers into this voyeuristic position. It is a vantage point from which they may view much but learn little.

In these late novels Lawrence is led away by doctrinaire considerations. He uses the novel as a vehicle for ideas. His explicit statements are insufficiently absorbed into his dramatic presentation. However, he never lost his mastery over forms more restricted. And so we are faced, in his last decade, with this paradox: that in the 1920s, concurrently with his worst novels, Lawrence produced some of his finest works; not only stories and poems but writings in prose that are less immediately classifiable.

6 Travel, Philosophy, Criticism, Prophecy

Twilight in Italy (1916); *Psychoanalysis and the Unconscious* (1921); *Movements in European History* (1921); *Sea and Sardinia* (1921); *Fantasia of the Unconscious* (1922); *Studies in Classic American Literature* (1923); *Reflections on the Death of a Porcupine* (1925); *Mornings in Mexico* (1927); *Pornography and Obscenity* (1929); *Assorted Articles* (1930); *À Propos of Lady Chatterley's Lover* (1930); *Apocalypse* (1931); *Etruscan Places* (1932); *Phoenix* (1936); *The Symbolic Meaning* (1962); *Phoenix II* (1968)

One cannot classify the non-fictional prose of Lawrence into neat compartments; not even the compartment called non-fiction. There is literary criticism in his travel sketches and philosophy in his criticism. The popular journalism of his later career often intensified into prophecy; the prophecy that characterizes the last stage of his life is criticism of a very high order indeed. As much as his verse, Lawrence's prose is the record of a flow of thought; and, as with his verse, components can be separated from the surrounding plasm and discussed as independent entities.

Lawrence's masters in his youth included Tolstoy, George Eliot and Dickens. And nowhere is the influence of Dickens more evident than in Lawrence's first impressions of Germany and Italy. There is the same mixture of descriptive comment and anecdote that could be encompassed only by a true novelist. Consider Dickens's description of the puppet-show at Genoa depicting Bonaparte imprisoned on St Helena: 'it was the finest spectacle I ever beheld, to see his body bending over the volume, like a bootjack, and his sentimental eyes glaring obstinately into the pit' (*Pictures from Italy*). A kindred vivaciousness suffuses

Lawrence's *Twilight in Italy*. Consider the essay on 'The Theatre' which portrays Enrico Persevalli, unemployed chemist, as Hamlet: 'He had become a hulking fellow, crawling about with his head ducked between his shoulders, pecking and poking, creeping about after other people, sniffing at them, setting traps for them, absorbed by his own self-important self-consciousness. His legs, in their black knee-breeches, had a crawling, slinking look . . .' *Twilight in Italy* was written substantially in February, April and October 1913, and appears to have emerged originally as a number of semi-independent travel sketches, very much successors of Lawrence's own impressions of Metz, Bavaria and the Tyrol. Indeed, the first essay in the book, 'The Crucifix Across the Mountains' (1915), is an inspired adaptation of the 'Christs in the Tirol' essay composed three years earlier. The original description of the different wayside shrines and effigies seen in a walk from Munich down to Merano is rewritten in such a way as to emphasize the different racial characteristics of the various peoples along the road. Bavaria affects one style of Christ, a peasant 'of middle age, plain, crude'; the banks of the Austrian Isar another, a 'small hewn Christ, the head resting on the hand'; while, on the road to Rome, Lawrence finds an elegant Christus like 'Gabriele D'Annunzio's son posing as a martyred saint'.

Further, the marvellous eye that saw these images and set them down so graphically went on in *Sea and Sardinia* (1921) to observe characters in their settings acutely enough to bring about Lawrence's most unified travel-book. The skein of narrative which only a novelist could have contrived is strung with descriptive brilliances. A peasant in Cagliari struts like a magpie in his 'full-sleeved white shirt and the close black bodice of thick, native frieze, cut low . . .'. Station officials drinking their soup in the café at Mandas turn into an operatic trio: 'Black-cap was the baritone; good rolling spoon-sucks. And the one in spectacles was the bass: he gave sudden deep gulps. All was led by the long trilling of the *maialino* . . .' And the humour and the observation that irradiate *Sea and Sardinia* illumine also the portrait of Maurice Magnus which forms the Introduction to that person's *Memoirs of the Foreign Legion* (1922).

This is one of the least-read of Lawrence's major writings. In

many ways it deserves to be set beside his tales. It is a characterization in depth of a confidence trickster *malgré lui*:

He looked like a man of about forty, spruce and youngish in his
deportment, very pink-faced, and very clean, very natty, very alert, like a
sparrow painted to resemble a tom-tit . . . 'That's been my philosophy all
my life; when you've got no money, you may as well spend it . . .'

This colourful figure is posed against some striking back-cloths:
post-war Florence with its shortage of food and high price of drink;
the monastery of Monte Cassino up in the mountains south of
Rome; Taormina, 'amethystine-glamorous', where Lawrence
lived for some time in Sicily; and 'a quiet, forlorn little yellow
street' in the suburbs of Valletta, the capital of Malta. Here
Magnus died by his own hand and beyond his means. His last
words in a note he left behind him were, 'I want to be buried first
class, my wife will pay.' But the whole memoir deserves to be set
among Lawrence's classics.

The travel sketches are at their best when they are least
ambitious. *Mornings in Mexico* (1924–25), for example, is
basically very Dickensian: it is a series of walks. On Friday
morning Lawrence tells us he tried to write but was distracted by
the parrots making a mockery of the dog ('Corasmin and the
Parrots'). On Saturday morning he went to the market and found
himself among black-hatted Indians from the hills and *sarape* men
who whistled like ferocious birds ('Market Day'). On Sunday
morning the sunshine drew him out of town and into the hills for a
picnic under the guava trees ('Walk to Huayapa'). And on
Monday morning his servant Rosalino – who had seemed quite
happy on the Sunday walk – decided to leave for his native village.
'He gave off a black steam of hate, that filled the *patio* and made
one feel sick . . .' ('The Mozo'). All these 'mornings' were written
in December 1924.

But there were more considered essays dating from the April
and the August of that year. They include 'Indians and Entertain-
ment' and the much admired 'Hopi Snake Dance'. These,
however, tend to obscure the simple lineaments of the book and
add to it an unwelcome layer of pretension. 'The American-Indian
sees no division into Spirit and Matter, God and not-God . . .'

Even in the first travel-book, *Twilight in Italy*, the process of revision was not altogether a happy one. Some of the sketches of 1913 were given a tremendous going-over in the summer and the early autumn of 1915. Though 'The Crucifix across the Mountains' emerged triumphant from revision, the vivacious observation in the sketch about the Theatre was interspersed with heavy second thoughts concerned with the Christian Infinite at the Renaissance – 'absorbed, dissolved, diffused into the great Not-Self . . .' The final version of 'The Lemon Gardens' in revision found its enchanting imagery of lakes and pillars hung about with weighty considerations of the Two Infinites. Later in his life Lawrence was to find contexts that gave concreteness to such meditations; but here, as elsewhere, the attempts at conceptualization fight against the colour and specificity of the travel books.

The years between *Twilight in Italy* and *Mornings in Mexico* saw the march of a series of tracts, not large in scale but amorphous in form, which Lawrence generically called his 'philosophy'. The years 1914–19, in particular, formed a period of mounting bitterness when practically everything he wrote was liable to be invaded by this curiously contextless manner of writing. He was confined to England by the war, and such work may well have proved a defence mechanism.

By no means all this 'philosophy' got published in its period. *A Study of Thomas Hardy* (1914), for example, did not appear (apart from its third chapter) until 1936, when *Phoenix*, a collection of Lawrence's papers, was brought out. The *Study*, like several of its successors, lacks coherent shape. Indeed, the most cogent remark that can be made about it is that its title seems a misnomer. Nisbet & Co. had commissioned a little book on Hardy for a series intended for students, and they must have been sorely puzzled by what they received. At any rate, they refused to publish it. One must say that, when the *Study* condescends to discuss Hardy, it does so to some effect; picking out the central figures of his books with sharp particularity. This, however, was not the line that Lawrence's criticism was to take; it contrasts greatly with the theoretic overtones that lend resonance to most of the later critical writing. Consider his account in the *Study* of *The Return of the Native*. Eustacia Vye is said to have a romantic imagination bounded by Paris and the *beau monde*; Wildeve is always attracted from outside and never driven from within; while Clym Yeobright thought his map of the static surface was the thing itself. Contrast this with the interpretation of Harold Child, who wrote the book that replaced Lawrence's in the series. He turns the novel into a species of novelette: 'Clym Yeobright is left alive, indeed, after Eustacia and Wildeve have been whirled by desire to death . . . but his suffering and humiliation had been terrible . . .' Clearly Child's prose wasn't up to interpreting Hardy's novel. That of Lawrence certainly was; but it is necessary to add that his particular exposition is confined mainly to Chapter III, the chapter that got published independently, and that the *Study* as a whole is best read as Lawrence's attempt to work out the elements of his 'philosophy'.

He begins the *Study* with a thunderous attack on various systems in society that, he considers, prevent man from attaining the fulfilment of his nature. He goes on to propound, as a positive value, a reconciliation between the sexes. As ever with Lawrence, the particulars he adduces by way of illustration – his sense of joy in the simple life of the poppy – come across sharply. The statements about Being and Not-Being, however, do not. And the more positive those statements are, the weaker they seem.

The positives are vague, too, in the *Study's* immediate successor, *The Crown* (1914–15). They achieve a partial realization only in certain images, such as this, of the Woman:

She is the doorway, she is the gate to the dark eternity of power, the creator's power. When I put my hand on her, my heart beats with a passion of fear and ecstasy, for I touch my own passing away, my own ceasing-to-be, I apprehend my own consummation in a darkness which obliterates me in its infinity. My veins rock as if they were being destroyed, the blood takes fire on the edge of oblivion, and beats backward and forward . . .

But this is not reducible to conceptual argument and is, in any case, better located in *The Rainbow*, where such philosophy, if that is what it is, finds a more concrete referent in terms of fictional character:

His blood beat up in waves of desire. He wanted to come to her, to meet her. She was there, if he could reach her. The reality of her who was just beyond him absorbed him. Blind and destroyed, he pressed forward, nearer, nearer, to receive the consummation of himself, be received within the darkness which should swallow him and yield him up to himself . . . She was the doorway to him, he to her . . .

This is the way in which Lawrence presents the reconciliation and mutual recognition of Tom Brangwen and his Polish wife, Lydia. It is the psychological notation that acts as a further resonance overlaying a fictional event, a specific encounter. It could also act as a footnote to *The Crown*. But *The Rainbow* does not need *The Crown*: it is a dramatic fiction, self-sufficient. On the other hand, *The Crown* would be incomprehensible without *The Rainbow*; and to that extent it is a failure. One has to wonder at the struggle to forge a terminology: the two eternities of Lion (passion, anger, masculinity) and Unicorn (peace, virginity, womanhood); and the Rainbow which, like the Holy Ghost, links them up. The Crown for which they fight is an advanced version of the reconciliation that Lawrence called for in *A Study of Thomas Hardy*: a mode of 'perfect relatedness'. But it seems to me that this is an abstraction from the conflict and reconciliation that Lawrence actively demonstrates in his novels and tales. And what I have said here seems to me true of all Lawrence's 'philosophy', at least until the concerted attempt of the mid-twenties to formulate ideas about the novel – which, in its turn, gave rise to the sustained consideration of society and myth in his final period.

The conceptual works of the First World War and its aftermath are a kind of crypto-fiction: a criticism without texts, a series of disquisitions starved of concrete reference. It is this that makes one prefer the decent pot-boiling of Lawrence's schoolbook, *Movements in European History* (1918–19), to the effervescing rhetoric of 'Love', 'Life' and 'The Reality of Peace' (1916–17).

One can find indications of specific experience in certain of these works, and this it is that gives them what being they have. In *The Education of the People* (1918, 1920), for instance, Lawrence's practical knowledge as a teacher powers his shrewder observations. One particularly warms to his remarks upon the position of the schoolteacher crushed between the educational theorists above him and the doggedly resisting pupils below. Yet the problem is given to us far more graphically in the narrative of

Ursula's conflict with both her headmaster and her classes in Chapter XIII of *The Rainbow*. Further, for all its incidental insights, *The Education of the People* is more than a little bedevilled by the peculiar psychology Lawrence worked out between its first drafting in 1918 and its final version in 1920. Practical hits at fallacies like Equality and Self-Expression come to us trailing cloudy trophies such as this:

at the great solar plexus an infant *knows*, in primary, mindless knowledge; and from this centre he acts and reacts directly, individually, and self-responsibly. The same from the cardiac plexus, and the two corresponding ganglia, lumbar and thoracic . . .

This occurs in *The Education of the People*, but it is the terminology of *Psychoanalysis and the Unconscious* (1920) and *Fantasia of the Unconscious* (1921). These represent a reaction against the psychology of Freud with its emphasis on sex and the incest-motive. Lawrence tried to counter Freud by propounding a psychology of his own based upon an equally individual view of physiology. He argued that there were four major nerve centres in the body. The thoracic ganglion related to the spine and shoulders and was associated with matters intellectual. The lumbar ganglion related to the spine and buttocks and was concerned with excretion and rejection. The cardiac plexus related to the nipples and was associated with breathing, eyesight and, by extension, concern for others. The solar plexus was the basis of the sensual life of man and was the seat of instinct.

Indeed, it was instinct largely that guided Lawrence's classification. For example, his feeling about the solar plexus is based on his sense of the intimate connexion between mother and child via the umbilical cord. The solar plexus is the seat of a creative knowledge to be valued more highly than the cerebral sort of knowledge associated with the thoracic ganglion. And the theory has, in Lawrence's hands, a certain beauty. But it is spoiled by his intermittent insistence that it is exact science, to be taken literally. The nerve centres that he specifies are four out of many which have to do with the activities he denotes, and it is clear that in all these activities he considerably underestimates the role of the brain.

Fantasia of the Unconscious philosophizes this physio-psychological theory and takes it to extremes. Most people, it asserts, are incapable of bringing their nerve-centres into relation with each other and with the universe. Therefore leaders must be evolved who would be responsible for the masses. There would be no need for the masses to read, to take decisions or even to be acquainted with the biological facts of sex. And so on. It is plain to see how this links up with the so-called leadership novels: *Aaron's Rod*, *Kangaroo*, *The Plumed Serpent*. This gives place, in the *Fantasia*, to a personal cosmography acting upon the analogy of the body, with the sun at the centre, vivifying and being vivified by its subordinates.

This could all be taken as a myth conveying perceptions that are too intuitive to be handled by conceptual prose. But what is wrong with *Psychoanalysis and the Unconscious* and *Fantasia of the Unconscious* is that they are insufficiently mythopoeic. One felt example does a good deal more by way of demonstration than a statement of opinion, no matter how frenetic that statement of opinion may be. But in these works there is a paucity of felt example.

Later philosophical disquisition uses images of animal life to illustrate its theme. And it is to those images we return; not to the disquisition at large. 'Reflections on the Death of a Porcupine' (1925) is an attempt to justify man's need to kill in order to hold his place in the universe. But it is the portrait of the porcupine that lives: 'a great aureoled tick . . . a pallid living bush . . . his white spoon-tail spiked with bristles . . .' Similarly, 'Love Was Once a Little Boy' (1925) attempts to put forward a concept of individualism – an individualism that is not merely egotistic. The prose strains and cracks in the attempt, and the one effective part of the essay is the unforgettable portrait of Susan – not as the embodiment of this individualism, but as Lawrence's wilful domestic cow. She 'flings her sharp, elastic haunch in the air with a kick and flick, and plunges off . . . her udder swinging like a chime of bells . . .'. Portraits like the Porcupine and Black-Eyed Susan really belong to *Birds, Beasts and Flowers* (see Chapter 9). It is strange Lawrence did not realize that he had already shown in those poems what he was endeavouring to conceptualize in 'Reflections on the Death of a Porcupine' and its attendant essays.

These essays evolved from American territory, but Lawrence had been interested in America long before he set foot there. The great American writers, especially Walt Whitman and Fenimore Cooper, had been a formative influence in his boyhood. During his enforced sojourn in England through the war years he began to think of the United States as a sort of promised land (see, for example, Letters, 27 July 1917). Lawrence started to draft a book on American literature and came to believe that the chapters might prove the basis of an American lecture tour. But, as it stands, *The Transcendental Element in American Literature* (1917–18) is a very different work from the one that ultimately transpired. Like *A Study of Thomas Hardy*, *The Transcendental Element* embodies literary criticism of a high order. However, it is criticism that put a constraint on Lawrence's perceptions and which, as an approach, was later abandoned. There can be no doubt that the final versions, published as *Studies in Classic American Literature*, form decidedly the more important book.

The essay on *Moby Dick* that appears in *The Transcendental Element* declares that the whale is symbolic, but it never faces what the whale is symbolic of. It propounds a paradox – the whale is sympathetic and yet to be hunted – but never resolves that paradox. This earlier essay takes leave of its subject suavely but also evasively: 'so ends one of the strangest and most wonderful books in the world'. But in what inheres this strangeness and wonder – *The Transcendental Element* cannot tell us that.

The essay that appears in *Studies in Classic American Literature* also begins by asking the question 'a symbol – of what?' But it goes on, through an astonishing series of asseverations, to answer it.

What then is Moby Dick? He is the deepest blood-being of the white race; he is our deepest blood-nature.

And he is hunted, hunted, hunted by the maniacal fanaticism of our white mental consciousness. We want to hunt him down. To subject him to our will. And in this maniacal conscious hunt of ourselves we get dark races and pale to help us, red, yellow, and black, east and west, Quaker and fire-worshipper, we get them all to help us in this ghastly maniacal hunt which is our doom and our suicide.

This is, among other things, an acting out of the psychological theories which were adumbrated in *Psychoanalysis* and *Fantasia*. It shows the cerebral will hunting down the sensory instinct. But it shows this in terms of *Moby Dick*: a powerful myth embodied in a great novel. The novel provides a context for the theory; the theory is a crucial interpretation of the novel. This indicates one reason why Lawrence's criticism is more telling than his earlier philosophy. But it also suggests that Lawrence's criticism is of a very curious kind. For one thing, it is exceedingly rare for a critic to be as great a writer as most of those he discusses: comparable, that is to say, with Fenimore Cooper, Hawthorne, Melville and Whitman. The activity of revision, from *The Transcendental Element in American Literature* to *Studies in Classic American Literature*, is a matter of Lawrence putting himself beside his topics. He writes, not as an interpreter expounding a master, but as an equal discussing an equal.

It is this that gives Lawrence's criticism an ostensibly informal appearance; unliterary, even polemical. He makes use of other writers to project his own vision, and it is the vision of a prophet rather than an aesthete. His greatest work in this genre dates from the mid-twenties onward, when most of his major creative effort was past. But, if we take a relatively early example, we can see how the mode came about.

The essay on Thomas Mann (1913) has often been termed unfair to its distinguished subject. Undoubtedly Lawrence is idiosyncratic and uses his texts in a manner calculated to advance his own concerns rather than those of Thomas Mann. What he has done is assimilate the German author to a concept of 'art for art's sake'. *Der Tod in Venedig* becomes, in this context of argument, an exploration of sickness whose main validity is the skill with which it is done. Lawrence's essay exists to define a kind of novel, the kind which exists as

craving for form in fiction, that passionate desire for the mastery of the medium of narrative, that will of the writer to be greater than and undisputed lord over the stuff he writes, which is figured to the world in Gustave Flaubert.

It is plain to see how this formulation influenced F. R. Leavis, who may well first have read it *in situ*, in *The Blue Review*. Lawrence here defines the kind of novel that he himself refused to write. Yet we may have doubts about the formulation. Something deeper than the question of aestheticism is involved. One can see Lawrence's prophetic tendency intensifying the definition beyond what is possible here if we look at later essays in criticism. Somerset Maugham, for example, is taken to task (1928) for the creation of characters for no other purpose than to show how excellently the author is able to observe imbecilities. H. G. Wells is held (1926) to pursue an art essentially egotistic, when the author obtrudes and occupies the space where his story should be.

In his major criticism, Lawrence is concerned to make a distinction between the author's intuition and his mind. He usually expresses the former in terms of the work itself or of the world which it describes. The latter is usually expressed in terms of the pressures of society, economics, the general average of the human masses.

A representative statement, even though the terminology is not as achieved as it might be, is the essay on John Galsworthy (1927). The basic material of *The Man of Property* is applauded: Galsworthy has described beings merely social, the Forsytes. They have no process of existence other than the scraping together of money; they are parasites upon life. But, Lawrence goes on, the author has falsified his intention. He puts forward, as an alternative by which to judge the Forsytes, the love affair of Irene and Bosinney. Irene, however, is a parasite even upon the parasites; while Bosinney is no more than an anti-Forsyte, a rebel whose rebellion can be described only in Forsytean terms as a grudge against property. It is as though, in launching a satire against the Forsytes, Galsworthy finds nothing but Forsytes in the wide human world. The artist's intuition has succumbed to his mind; a mind formed by the pressures of the surrounding society.

What Lawrence is particularly against, in life as in letters, is the mind as social entity. In a fragment to be found in *Phoenix*, a kind of emission from the Galsworthy essay, he writes, 'The moment the human being becomes conscious of himself, he ceases to be himself.' Lawrence works out this aperçu in terms of authors and characters alike. For example, there is a penetrating review (1927) of *The Social Basis of Consciousness* by Trigant Burrow. This is a

book well worth reading in itself: it advocates group therapy and
the importance of developing a tactile consciousness. Lawrence's
crucial comment is this: 'The real trouble lies in the inward sense
of "separateness" which dominates every man.' He claims that
man has made a 'picture' of himself – what, in other contexts,
Lawrence calls a 'social being' – and that this picture relates to
living reality as a two-dimensional pocket-camera photograph
relates to the person it claims to portray. In other words,
Lawrence puts forward a distinction between the intuition which is
in touch with the universe and the 'social being' which is a prisoner
of its own society.

Lawrence's positive position is defined even further in a
remarkable series of essays written in 1925. They benefit by being
studied together. 'Surgery for the Novel – or a Bomb' criticizes the
so-called realism to be found in such novelists as Joyce and Proust.
This, for Lawrence, is yet another example of the novelist acting as
mind; the social form of ego. It is also liable to give rise to a
restricted form of moralism: this development Lawrence discusses
in another essay in the series, 'Art and Morality'. Here he defines
such moralism as an inability to see things as living by their own
laws; it imposes on them a kind of Platonic Idea 'in all its
photographically developed perfection'.

As an antidote to all this Lawrence puts forward serious claims
for a kind of novel other than that written by Joyce and Proust. He
sees it as 'a perfect medium for revealing to us the changing
rainbow of our living relationships' ('Morality and the Novel').
His word is 'medium' as distinct from 'moral'; for the kind of novel
he admires resists philosophy. 'You can develop an instinct for
life, if you will, instead of a theory of right and wrong' ('Why the
Novel Matters'). In yet another of these related essays, 'The Novel
and the Feelings', Lawrence carries the distinction further; seeing
the reader not as listening to the 'didactic statements' of the
author but to the 'calling cries' of the characters. In other words,
the work of the reader as well as the author is to attend to what is
there; and this, in contradistinction to the mind which bends living
reality into set patterns, is intuition. This is the attitude implied in
Lawrence's frequent references to the novel as a live being.
Therefore it is not surprising to find in an essay called simply 'The

Novel' a claim that this form, at least in Lawrence's vision of it, is the highest mode of human expression so far attained. Further, in explaining his vision of the novel, Lawrence reiterates his central proposition on behalf of intuition against mind: 'the novel . . . is incapable of the absolute'.

These essays are very much literary theory: one may feel the need for more examples of writing in practice. However, in more clearly practical criticism, Lawrence's judgments tend to be pejorative. For example, he claims that Emma and Charles Bovary are too insignificant as characters to carry the full weight of Flaubert's 'profound sense of tragedy'. And the Russians, by whom Lawrence seems especially to mean Dostoyevsky, 'escape the non-heroic dilemma of our age by making every man his own introspective hero'. These remarks are culled from an essay (1922) on the Sicilian novelist, Giovanni Verga; the better of the two versions is in *Phoenix II*. And it is Verga whom Lawrence sees as a modern classic; a classic, that is to say, in an age that fights against the existence of such things. For Lawrence, Verga seems to be doing all that is possible, given the quality of the time at which he lived (1840–1922). He sees Verga as facing up to 'the non-heroic dilemma of our age'. He feels that Verga creates in his Mastro-Don Gesualdo a figure with such positive attributes as energy, sagacity and humaneness. Gesualdo is a peasant whose positive qualities make him a power in the land. Unfortunately, the land is a mean one. Gesualdo is brought down by the age; he does not compare with the Greek heroes; he has no gods or goddesses to fix his imagination. 'Even his Greek ambitious desire to come out splendidly, with a final splendid look of the thing and a splendid final ring of words, turns bitter. The Sicilian aristocracy was an infinitely more paltry thing than Gesualdo himself. It is the tragedy of a man who is forced to be ordinary because all his visions have been taken away from him.'

Nevertheless, Lawrence thinks *Mastro-Don Gesualdo* is as good a novel as we are likely to get in our unheroic time. His own translation (1922) is one of the most sustained and colourful of his writings; it also acts as a formidable piece of backing criticism. To read Lawrence's translation is to become convinced of Giovanni Verga's greatness. And no more persuasive support for

Lawrence's appreciation of Verga can be found than his version of the death of Gesualdo:

But once there, among his own possessions, he realized that it was actually all over, that every hope was lost, for nothing mattered to him any more. The vines were already coming into leaf, the young corn was high, the olives in flower, the sumachs green, and over everything a mist was spread, a gloom, a black veil. The house itself, with its windows shut, and the terrace where Bianca and his daughter used to sit and work, the deserted avenue, even his own country people who were afraid of bothering him and kept at a distance, there in the courtyard or under the shed, everything wrung his heart; everything said to him: 'What are you doing? What do you want . . .?'

It reads, in Lawrence's translation, like the work of a Hardy who chose a Sicilian terrain. But this is a Hardy who, unlike the subject of the *Study*, Lawrence was able to see as standing with the exception against the average. It is a Hardy who represents the individual interest against the interests of the community as a whole; and this, for Lawrence, is an advantage. Verga may not have, says Lawrence, the mythopoeia with which Homer and Sophocles invested their heroes, but he has far more sense of the heroic than Hardy; or than Tolstoy, Flaubert and Dostoyevsky.

This sense of the heroic thwarted by the meanness of modern society runs through and links together Lawrence's late tracts. Predominantly they are concerned with matters of sex, literature and censorship. He claims that a movement against the instincts took the form of a morality in all countries after the inception of syphilis ('Introduction to These Paintings', 1928). He finds in Cézanne, however, an instinctual intuition akin to that which he applauds in Verga. 'He wished to displace our present mode of mental-visual consciousness, the consciousness of mental concepts, and substitute a mode of consciousness that was predominantly intuitive, the awareness of touch.' Here, again, we have the contrast between knowing and being, between the mind and the intuition. The fear of touch and of being touched resulted, says Lawrence, in a kind of Puritanism which condemned as obscenity the natural flow of sex and which censored as pornography its celebration in literature and art. 'The greatest of all lies in the modern world is the lie of purity and the dirty little secret.

The grey ones left over from the nineteenth century are the embodiment of this lie. They dominate in society, in the press, in literature, everywhere . . . which means, of course, perpetual censorship of anything that would militate against the lie of purity and the dirty little secret . . .' ('Pornography and Obscenity', 1929). The banning of *Lady Chatterley's Lover* and its subsequent dissemination at the hands of pirates gave Lawrence a brilliant opportunity to expatiate upon this theme. In 'À Propos of *Lady Chatterley's Lover*' (1929) he traces the Puritan heresy back to a past far predating that of Sir William Joynson-Hicks who condemned his paintings. It predated even the Elizabethans who cowered and sniggered before the onset of syphilis. 'Buddha, Plato, Jesus, they were all three utter pessimists as regards life, teaching that the only happiness lay in abstracting oneself from life, the daily, yearly, seasonal life of birth and death and fruition, and in living in the "immutable" or eternal spirit.'

Lawrence saw that it was going to take more than the novels of Verga, more even than his own novels, to restore communication. He came to believe that it was possible to re-achieve the ancient forms of mythology that lived before the grand idealists, Buddha, Plato and Jesus, cut us off from our roots. In 'À Propos of *Lady Chatterley's Lover*', a work far greater than the novel it defends, Lawrence took the mode of criticism a very long way indeed; towards prophecy, the philosophy-in-a-context so different from the unfocused moralizing, the 'philosophy' of the war years. This prophecy is very individual, an emanation of Lawrence's last phase. There are signs of this even in the pieces that he wrote for the newspapers, many collected as *Assorted Articles*, mostly produced between May and December 1928. Instances that come to mind are 'Nobody Loves Me', 'We Need One Another', 'The State of Funk' and 'The Real Thing'. It can be seen, too, in the Introduction (1930) to his translation (with Koteliansky) of 'The Grand Inquisitor', that 'poem' which is one of the climactic points of *The Brothers Karamazov*. Lawrence sees this as an essential criticism of Christ, that Christianity is too difficult for the mass of mankind. 'The Grand Inquisitor' (whom Lawrence identifies with Dostoyevsky himself) 'finds that to be able to live at all, mankind must be loved more tolerantly and more contemptuously than

Jesus loved it . . . loved for itself, for what it is, and not for what it ought to be . . .'. Lawrence builds this criticism into a positive by invoking what he takes to be past forms of mythopoeia. The loci classici for this are two great works of his final years, *Etruscan Places* and *Apocalypse*.

In *Etruscan Places* (1927) Lawrence sketches the life of the people who flourished before the mechanistic Romans and the idealistic Christians. He sees the Etruscans as a people who developed neither gods nor nationhood; who kept life fluid and changing; whose pictures on the walls were an evocation of all we have lost. 'Here, in this faded Etruscan painting, there is a quiet flow of touch that unites the man and the woman on the couch, the timid boy behind, the dog that lifts his nose, even the very garlands that hang from the wall.' The tombs are badly damaged, and yet they are full of hints and suggestions. The spoliation and blur are actually turned to account. Half in inspired inference, half in fiction, Lawrence makes his tour. Further, the lightness and colour of his prose turn what might have been a funereal topic into a celebration. The Etruscan memory survives as a quick ripple of life – 'Fragments of people at banquets, limbs that dance without dancers, birds that fly in nowhere, lions whose devouring heads are devoured away . . .!' The archaeology may be hypothetical, but the prose is instinct with energy and life.

Likewise, a hypothetical text gave rise to the other great positive myth in this last stage of Lawrence's life. In 1924 he had reviewed an ingenious reconstruction by John Oman of the Book of Revelation. Dr Oman's edition attempted to clarify the text in terms of Christianity, but it suggested to Lawrence that other inferences were possible. His interest was also quickened through his association with Frederick Carter from 1923 onwards. Carter's manuscript on the subject of Revelation resulted in Lawrence writing two introductions to what eventually became Carter's book, *The Dragon of Revelation*. But neither introduction was used for its original purpose. One (January 1930) was published as an independent essay in *The London Mercury*; the other (December 1929) became a separate book, *Apocalypse*.

Lawrence claims that the Book of Revelation was originally a pagan text and that it had been rewritten several times. The apocalypticists before the time of Christ sought to bring it into line with Jewish scriptures; St John of Patmos revised it into his kind of Christianity; and Christian scribes adapted St John's text in order to make it even more orthodox and fit to be accepted as part of the Bible. In *Apocalypse* Lawrence peels off these layers of adaptation in an attempt to reveal the original form of the mythology. Its main characteristics, he suggests, are that it was in contact with the cosmos; that it was a cult of vitality and potency; that it concerned itself with the living things of life now and not – as Christianity tends to – with the hereafter. In particular, Lawrence sees the woman 'clothed with the sun' in Chapter 12 as the original focus of the whole myth. She is a figure alien equally to Jews and to Christians; a kind of cosmic Mother 'magnificent with her golden cup of the wine of sensual pleasure in her hand'. But the Apocalypse shows her driven out, into the desert. 'She has been in the desert ever since, the great cosmic mother crowned with all the signs of the zodiac. Since she fled, we have had nothing but virgins and harlots, half-women: the half-women of the Christian era.' Through his evocation of this figure as a positive concept Lawrence points to all we have lost in the world. How, we ask, can we get in touch with life again? Lawrence answers with almost the last words he was to write. They come at the end of *Apocalypse*. 'Start with the sun, and the rest will slowly, slowly happen.'

Apocalypse is a form of criticism that has intensified into prophecy. Just as in earlier work Lawrence differentiated between the integrity of the material and the will of the author, so here he shows how the vision of a pagan universe can be overlaid and obscured by a mechanistic system. Even if we do not accept his interpretation, we may find that it serves to alert and focus some of the dissatisfactions we feel with the society about us. It may even help us towards our own positive re-assessment.

In some of his works Lawrence discovered mythologies through travel: observing the open-air life of the Sicilian peasant and the ritual dances of the Mexicans, and visiting the ruined Etruscan tombs. In other works he traverses a text: 'the bright book of the novel', Melville, Verga, the Apocalypse. And, in their turn, all these prose works, whether travel or criticism, link up with those most astonishing revelations of his genius: the later Tales.

7 Tales (1911, 1921–27)

The Ladybird (1923); *St Mawr* (1925); *The Woman Who Rode Away* (1928); *The Escaped Cock* (1929); *The Virgin and the Gipsy* (1930)

There is a form of fiction which has given rise to some of the best work in English. Yet it has no agreed name. Variously it is called the long short story, the conte, nouvelle, novella or the tale. For no especial reason it is this last name that I shall use in discussing Lawrence's work in the genre.

A tale is larger in scope than a short story but more restricted in compass than a novel. The distinction, so far as Lawrence is concerned, can be made fairly tersely. Lawrence's tale 'The Ladybird' was developed from a short story of 1915, 'The Thimble'. The earlier work shows the homecoming of a husband wounded in the First World War. But he and his wife knew each other so little before they were married that they meet now almost as strangers. Indeed, his wound has changed him so much that, in effect, they have to start all over again. The story is a fine naturalistic study, but it has not quite assimilated its raw material. For instance, a central incident is the wife's finding an old gold thimble in the sofa; the husband eventually throws it away. 'Who would give the gift of a gold thimble set with jewels, in the year 1801? Perhaps it was a man come home from the wars . . .' The disposal of the thimble may symbolize a jettisoning of the past. But the interpretation is not clear-cut. The thimble has an emotive vibration in excess of anything that it can be shown to stand for.

On this foundation Lawrence proceeded to build the fabric of the tale, 'The Ladybird' (1921). We still have the return of the wounded soldier to his waiting wife. But the thimble is given a history. The question of the earlier story, 'Who would give the gift . . .?', is answered in the tale. The thimble is made the property of a character original to 'The Ladybird': a German prisoner-of-war, the Bohemian Count Dionys Psanek. It is no vulgar jewelled artefact, as in the short story, but is finely wrought and bears the Count's emblem – a ladybird. And the ladybird itself, as an emblem, has a genealogy stretching back to the Egyptian scarab – a line that connects the Count with the Pharaohs. They, in their turn, took the scarab to be a symbol of the First Principle of creation. Its roots go far back, indeed.

The Count himself is the datum that is wanting in the short story. When the tale opens, the husband has not yet returned from the war and the Count is lying badly wounded in London. The line of imagery associated with the Count develops as he recovers. It conveys a dark and brooding presence – his black brows, particularly, are insisted upon. As he gains strength, he acquires an aura like that of Pluto, the legendary King of the Underworld. His statements are oracular, but instinct with poetry. '"The true fire is invisible . . . even the sun is dark. It is only his jacket of dust that makes him visible . . ."'

So far from being a thing anonymous, the thimble in the tale is a gift that the Count had passed on to the wife, Daphne, when she was a young girl. It is, as it were, his pledge, binding her to him. But circumstances – class, caste, the war – separated them. She had married fame; borne a stillborn child; and was ill, always ill. Her illness seems to stem from a passion that is thwarted.

Subtly the Count works upon this. It is not a seduction; rather, it is the awakening in her of a recognition that she is the feminine counterpart of what he finds in himself. '"True love is dark, a throbbing together in darkness, like the wild-cat in the night . . ."' There is a fire, as of a wild-cat, in her eyes as well as his. But the relationship does not come into full play until her husband comes home.

The husband's injury is much less severe than the dreadful wound sustained by his counterpart in 'The Thimble'. But it is symbolic of a contracted personality: the bright jacket of dust, so to speak. His love for Daphne is at once sensual and abstract; he desires, in effect, to be her slave. Significantly he calls her Iris, and Proserpine.

If she is Proserpine, most certainly Psanek, the outlaw, is Pluto. He is going away – she feels, into the dark – and, before he goes, spends a fortnight in her parents' house. This proves to be a kind of evocation of the old England now vanishing after the war. At night, when the Count feels quite alone, he sings to himself the folk-songs of his own dialect: one, in particular, about a swan that married a man but went back to her own kind. This has an application to the mismated Daphne; it draws her to him. But nothing, in the outward sense, happens. Daphne does not leave her husband and go with the Count: even though he, unlike her husband, can dominate her. The Count has prophesied the end of Europe and recognizes no future for himself upon the earth. His vision is a spiritual one: he sees himself as reigning after death in an Underworld where she will be his Queen. It is as though in the post-war world everyone is deracinated and as though that world itself is condemned. Only with its collapse will existence begin.

The tale exudes a terrible despair. Among other things, it is an elegy for the England that Lawrence had celebrated in earlier stories. Much of what the Count says, Lawrence wrote elsewhere, as his own opinion; though the doctrine gains enormously by being placed in the mouth of a specific character in a specific tale.

There are traces, and more than traces, of that England Lawrence thought lost in another of the great tales, 'The Fox' (1918, revised 1921). Like 'The Ladybird', 'The Fox' is written out of an acute sense of the war. But here Lawrence re-adopts his old panacea of salvation through individual relationships – in this world, not, as with 'The Ladybird', in the next. However, the salvation is more qualified than that found, say, as a positive in *Women in Love*.

'The Fox', like 'The Ladybird', has a connection with an earlier story. In this case it is a much more fugitive one, with 'You Touched Me'. Like that story, 'The Fox' concerns two young women living together, and the incursion into their lives of a young man. But, in the tale, these are emancipated women, and they work hard trying to run a small farm. They are known by their surnames and share almost a marital relationship. March, the more robust of the two, is the 'man about the place'. Banford has most of the money; is delicate; is in charge of the domestic side of affairs.

Their farm, however, fails. They cannot manage their cows and their hens are pillaged by a fox. This creature is finely created in the tale, both as a physical entity in himself and as a forerunner of the compelling male, Henry, who is to enter their lives. The sudden incursion of the latter is masterly. The animal aspect is brought across – 'His eyes were blue, and very bright and sharp. On his cheeks, on the fresh ruddy skin were fine, fair hairs, like a down, but sharper. It gave him a slightly glistening look.' He hypnotizes March in much the same way as the fox does, and she shrinks, trying not to be seen.

At first Banford treats Henry like a young brother. But she distrusts the development of his relationship with March. Banford makes a painful scene when he proposes to her partner. Thereafter, Banford puts herself in active competition with the young man. After Henry has returned to camp – he is a soldier – she gets March to write breaking off her engagement. He comes back at once, and resumes work as if he had never left off, continuing March's attempt to chop down a tree that Banford wants for the fire. It is an image of Banford herself: weak, leaning, sere. He warns Banford out of the way but adopts a manner that guarantees she will stay where she is. The tree falls on Banford, and she is killed.

Up to this point we have a precisely told story: naturalistic on the literal level, with symbolic overtones relating Henry with his glowing face to the fox and the cornered March to his quarry. The fox and Banford are his quarry in another sense: the smaller predators are overcome by the greater. But, with the death of Banford, the story modulates into a tone more lyrical and less actual, especially when it comes to describe March's emotions. 'She had to be like the seaweeds she saw as she peered down from the boat, swaying forever delicately under water, with all their delicate fibrils put tenderly out upon the flood . . .' One could say that this more abstract register of language indicates the sorrow of March for her friend, but it also shows that Lawrence has difficulty in reconciling himself to Henry's action. Does one sanction the removal of a human being as though she were an obstacle in the path? Lawrence represents the couple as being uneasy; is this enough? They are to go to Canada, but that, too, is something of an illusion. March 'can't tell what it will be like over there' and neither, so far as this tale is concerned, can Lawrence. So the tale comes to a rather uncertain halt.

No such uncertainty, however, causes fluctuation in 'The Captain's Doll' (1921). This tale also has a prototype, a story called 'The Mortal Coil' (1913). It is based on an anecdote of the Prussian army told by Frieda Lawrence's father. The main point of resemblance is that in both story and tale there is a young woman who is having an affair with a rather elusive army officer. Apart from this central datum there are a number of details in common: for example, each heroine has a close bond with a woman friend. In 'The Mortal Coil' the two girls are found dead in bed together, overcome by the smoke of a faulty stove. It is an anecdote, beautifully told, but amounting to no more than the observed particulars.

'The Captain's Doll', with not dissimilar basic material, develops very differently. Just as 'The Ladybird' added Count Dionys to the simple facts about the thimble, so this tale produces as its central concept the Doll. By making an image of a person, you reduce your idea of his personality to the size and absurdity of a puppet. In this way you gain power over his soul. The idea is familiar in witch-lore.

Here, the Countess Hannele is compelled to make dolls – all kinds of dolls – for a living. In a freak of spirit she makes a doll that is an image of her lover, a Scottish army captain, Alexander Hepburn. The doll in the tale is a comic object with its close-fitting tartan trousers, even down to 'that air of aloofness and perfect diffidence which marks an officer and a gentleman'.

This indicates the basic tone. The tale is a comedy – a comedy of male and female sexuality. Hannele's close friend Mitchka, on seeing the doll, says, '"That is him."' The Captain himself comments, '"You've got me."' His wife – for he is married – comes over from England to rescue him and tries in vain to purchase the doll, which by now has acquired a highly suggestive aura. '"It is a little – er – indelicate, don't you think?"' says Mrs Hepburn.

But she herself has made a doll of the Captain; a mental one. She tells the astonished Hannele that he kneeled to her on their wedding-night. This bears all too comic a resemblance to the initial presentation of the doll, head downwards with its arms tossed out. The visual caricature is also a moral one, and this is what Captain Hepburn seeks to avoid. He is detached from his wife, and, after she dies in mysterious circumstances, he detaches himself from Hannele also. Later he decides he wants her again; but, in the meantime, she has disappeared.

The tale ends with the reunion, insofar as they have ever been united, of Hannele and the Captain. This takes place, where he has tracked her down, in the Austrian Tyrol. He voices in a crucial dialogue the central idea of the tale; but behind the temperament of Hepburn is Lawrence's sense of the comedy of the sexes.

'If a woman loves you, she'll make a doll out of you. She'll never be satisfied till she's made your doll . . . And that's what love means. And so I won't be loved. And I won't love . . . I'll be honoured and I'll be obeyed: or nothing.'

'Then it'll most probably be nothing,' said Hannele sarcastically. 'For I assure you I've nothing but love to offer.'

The cleansing effect of the high mountains, away from the distractions of what passes for civilization; the natural attraction between these two temperamental people – this is what brings Hannele and the Captain together, if 'together' is the word. For the prospects are stormy – their wrangling assures us of that – even though the tale itself is a vivacious rendering of an adult relationship. Critics have read it rather solemnly; but 'The Captain's Doll' will not fall in the reader's estimation if he takes it as a comedy.

I have mentioned Lawrence's idea of the cleansing effect of the high mountains. This, or something of the sort, is the positive of 'The Woman Who Rode Away' (1924). Here Lawrence judges what he takes to be the decadence of European civilization. There was to be a crude parallel in 'None of That', a story of 1927. In this story, a wealthy American lady makes men dance upon her whims as though they were marionettes. But she falls in love at last with a Mexican toreador, representative of nothing so much as sheer animality. Not only does he reject her with contempt, but he hands her over to his bullring gang who communally rape her. To some extent prefiguring this is an uncompleted story – really the first chapter of a novel – 'The Wilful Woman' (1922). Here, another rich American lady travels West. Both these figures are based to some extent on Mabel Dodge Luhan, who had summoned Lawrence to New Mexico in order that he might write a book about Taos.

These unimportant stories are subsumed in 'The Woman Who Rode Away'. We are shown not only the woman's bondage, her marriage to a tedious mine-owner, but her arrested development. Curiosity leads her to ride into the mountains to seek out a tribe that was said to keep up the old religion of the Aztecs. The plot is slight, almost ballad-like, and much of its effect lies in Lawrence's power to evoke the mountains – 'stretches of naked rock against the sky, rock slashed already and brindled with white stripes of snow . . .'. For, in all essentials, the woman fulfils a tribal prophecy. This says that the Indians will regain their lost power over the sun when a white woman voluntarily offers herself as a sacrifice. The tribe takes her in and, after a period of ritual preparation, she is brought to a place of hollow rock facing an amphitheatre. Down the rock hangs a stalactite of ice. The woman is taken below the ice and made to lie on a large, flat stone. The aged cacique holds a knife.

In absolute motionlessness he watched till the red sun should send his ray through the column of ice. Then the old man would strike, and strike home, accomplish the sacrifice and achieve power.

The mastery that man must hold and that passes from race to race.

Whatever one feels about this ideology – it is substantially that of the far inferior *Plumed Serpent* – in context here the vision is clear and evocative. Lawrence, in satirizing Western corruption, sets out, as his positive, the primitive intensity of the wild spaces.

This is seen at fullest stretch in 'St Mawr' (1924). It is a more complex creation than 'The Woman Who Rode Away'. The story develops in eight phases, which are not, however, mutually exclusive.

For instance, the social satire which is basic to Phase 1 persists throughout the earlier half of the tale. But, as the tale develops, the satire is increasingly beset by other, more primitive, pressures. The satirical tone is set early on:

There was a marriage . . . Lou and Rico leased a little old house in Westminster, and began to settle into a certain layer of English society. Rico was becoming an almost fashionable portrait painter. At least, *he* was almost fashionable, whether his portraits were or not. And Lou too was almost fashionable: almost a hit. There was some flaw somewhere. In spite of their appearances, both Rico and she would never quite go down in any society. They were the drifting artist sort. Yet neither of them was content to be of the drifting artist sort. They wanted to fit in, to make good . . .

Lou Witt is the daughter of a rich American, deceased. She is, in this early phase of the tale, depicted as being a dreamer, a games-player. Rico is the son of an Australian senior civil servant, a baronet. He is seen throughout the tale as a tame animal – willing to wound and yet afraid to strike. It was clever of Lawrence to make both Lou and Rico, so far as English society was concerned, outsiders. As the tale progresses, the tame Rico more and more fits in, while the unawakened Lou recedes from society into life. It is this recession that is the positive of 'St Mawr'.

One active agent in Lou's recession is her mother. This widow, essentially critical, possesses all the force of frustration. Lawrence depicts her in terms of daggers and pistols. She advances on people as though demanding, 'Your virility or your life! Your femininity or your life!' As the tale progresses, it prefigures to some extent the late story 'Mother and Daughter', in which both females metaphorically sit upon a weak husband.

But the key agent in Lou's deliverance from European society is the horse, St Mawr. His introduction marks the beginning of the second phase of the tale. He is, more even than the Fox in the earlier tale, a physical presence in the narrative here. He is described in literal terms but there is also a symbolic aura about him – red-gold colour, sun-arched neck, glowing fearsome eyes, fire of the great ruddy body. Rico's response to all this is, ' "Such a marvellous colour! Almost orange! But rather large, I should say, to ride in the Park . . ." ' Really he would have preferred a car. He reluctantly accepts the great horse as a present, together with a groom – who, in every sense, goes with the horse. Superficially there is no resemblance: Lewis is a little scrub of a fellow. There are, however, deep fires within.

The horse proves untamable, at least by Rico. A crisis comes in the third phase of the tale. On an excursion to the Welsh hills, the horse shies. Rico panics and succeeds only in pulling St Mawr backwards on top of him. The incident is rendered graphically and physically through Lou's eyes. 'Then she saw a pale gold belly, and hoofs that worked and flashed in the air, and St Mawr writhing, straining his head terrifically upwards, his great eyes starting from the naked lines of his nose.'

Rico is furious. At first he wants to have the horse shot, but later he intends to sell him to a lady who will attempt to calm St Mawr down by having him gelded. This fixes a resolution Lou's mother, the formidable Mrs Witt, has already had in mind – to leave a Europe she despises and go to America, to the mountains. She and her daughter decide to take the horse with them, before Rico can sell him. They leave with the two grooms: Lewis, already mentioned, and the sexual, promiscuous Phoenix, an Arizona Indian.

This resolution begins Phase 4 which is otherwise dominated by the developing relationship between Mrs Witt and Lewis. Her insatiable curiosity has been aroused by his unapproachability; a quality he has in common with the horse. But her advances are rejected. This setback paralyses her will. She plays little part in the tale thereafter.

The fifth phase begins with the British Isles fading away – one of Lawrence's poignant farewells to England – and the transitory feeling as the ship crosses the Atlantic. It is notable that the transition is marked by the same properties, though in reverse order, that were to occur in Lawrence's haunting but unfinished tale, 'The Flying Fish' (1925). We see the flying fish near Havana. We also see the American tourists on shore, sporting name-plates in their lapels in case they get too drunk to find their way back to their hotels. There are, too, the porpoises in the Gulf of Mexico. Lou and her mother eventually arrive in Texas, and here, on a ranch, St Mawr settles down at last. He has, after all, performed his role in the tale. Now he diminishes into an ordinary horse making advances to the rancher's long-legged mare. Even the formerly intransigent groom Lewis is subdued and somewhat piqued by the cowboys and the open spaces – the sense of 'something new, something not used-up'.

If Phase 5 is transition, Phase 6 is definitely search. Here the mistress-groom relationship between Mrs Witt and Lewis gives way in the story to that between Lou and Phoenix. The latter's easy sexuality is rejected – '"I am not a lover nor a mistress nor a wife."' It is something other than this that Lou is looking for. No longer a dreamer, she is now on a quest. She goes to see a ranch in the high mountains. When she sees it, she says, '*"This is the place."*'

Like 'The Woman Who Rode Away', 'St Mawr' depends a great deal upon Lawrence's power of evoking natural beauty. The seventh phase of the tale relates the past history of the ranch and of the people who wrestled with the savage country here. It centres particularly on a rancher's wife from New England.

From her doorway, from her porch, she could watch the vast eagle-like wheeling of the daylight, that turned as the eagles which lived in the near rocks turned overhead in the blue, turning their luminous, dark-edged-patterned bellies and underwings upon the pure air, like winged orbs. So the daylight made the vast turn upon the desert, brushing the farthest outwatching mountains . . .

It seems to me that Lawrence's dynamic evocation of this alien landscape justifies his theme that here are the sources of energy lost to Europe. This phase as a whole seems to derive from the 'oceanic feeling', described by Freud in his *Civilization and its Discontents* as a sense of areas of emotion beyond the normal experience of the human psyche. But Lawrence's concept as acted out in his tale is more complex even than that of Freud. It is the struggle of the civilized being in an attempt to bring order to the 'oceanic' wilderness – 'the effort, the effort!' To this extent, the history of the New England lady anticipates what we may divine of Lou's future in New Mexico.

Therefore the eighth and final phase is, and needs to be, no more than a coda. We see Lou acquire the place. She says, '"I am here, right deep in America, where there's a wild spirit wants me, a wild spirit more than men."' In this way, Lou saves herself from what she terms the cheapness of modern sex and of modern civilization. It is interesting that she speaks of the mountains and the wilds almost in sexual terms, as an awakening, a salvation. One may feel that Lawrence himself thought like this, but, as with the utterances of Count Dionys in 'The Ladybird', the idea gains tremendously by being given to a specific person in a specific setting. Lawrence is essentially a particularist, which is why it is not very useful to seek to draw a general philosophy from his writings.

Lawrence uses the wilderness to quite another end in his tale 'The Princess' (1924). Dollie Urquhart, the eponymous heroine, is a protagonist less flexible than Lou Witt – and this, in part, is the point of the story. Dollie has been dubbed The Princess by her father who thinks that he is of royal blood. It is all part of a training which leads her to feel herself apart from humanity; even to despise it. The Princess has lived in the hot-house of her father's madness, and it is only after his death that she finds herself in the open air.

All the images associated with her suggest a clear, finished crystal; an artefact rather than a human being. She can settle nowhere: she is on the run from the world's vulgarities. At length she arrives at a ranch in New Mexico: the people there don't interest her, but she acquires a guide who takes her into the high mountains looking for deer. This is no ordinary guide: his family used to own the territory where now he works. He is associated with images that are physical, primitive, Indian – his eyes seem hopeless, yet in their depth is a spark of pride or self-confidence.

On the way to the mountains the Princess loses her female companion and she goes on alone with the guide, Romero. They stay overnight in a little cabin: she is in the bunk and Romero by the wall. But the night is cold and she calls him over to warm her. He makes love to her, but she – 'she had never, never wanted to be given over to this.' In the morning she is distant: she treats him as a thing and not as a man. He feels his manhood insulted and proceeds to keep her prisoner in the hut. She goes hard as ice with anger: '"You think you can conquer me this way. But you can't. You can never conquer me."'

Two men come out to find her. In the resultant struggle Romero is shot. But, after her experience, the Princess is never quite the same again. The bobbed hair is grey at the temples; the eyes are a little mad. What was a fulfilment for Lou has destroyed Dollie.

It may be agreed that there is no Romero in Lou's life. First St Mawr, and then the mountains, stand as a substitute. But the intrusive masculinity that is the destruction of the Princess is the

awakening of two other Lawrence heroines, Louisa Lindley and
Yvette Saywell.

The first version of 'The Daughters of the Vicar' (1911) is
contemporary with attractive but relatively juvenile work such as
'The Ballad of Another Ophelia', 'The Shades of Spring' and *The
White Peacock*. In its revised version (1913) the tale exhibits a
mastery of subject, form and language which few writers of prose
fiction have managed at such an early stage of their development.
It prefigures the great tales of the 1920s, not least in dramatizing
the conflict between refined virginity and the animality of primitive man. The vicar of the title is presented, together with his
family, in images of pallor, chill, repression, austerity. The elder
daughter has a fine profile, pale and distinguished, but she marries
a weak and deformed creature with the merits only of a safe
income and a prosperous living; another vicar. This is a foil to the
main theme which shows us the most physically inclined of the
family, the plump and obstinate Louisa, courting a coal miner.
They meet through the illness of his old mother. And Louisa finds
herself running the house, even down to scrubbing the miner's
back when he comes home from the pit. All this is intensely
physical, and, as such, anathema to the neuroses of the vicarage.
Indeed, the young couple have to emigrate to Canada, where
Lawrence was to send March and Henry in 'The Fox' and which
was intended as the original destination of Lady Chatterley and
her gamekeeper.

The tale is obviously symbolic, though it at no time loses hold of
the literal narrative. There is nothing in it as abstract as the last
pages of 'The Fox'. On the other hand, 'The Daughters of the
Vicar', fine tale though it is, does not achieve the richness and the
depth of 'The Virgin and the Gipsy' (1926).

Here, the rectory is a fascinating study of the inhibitions that
can exist in family life. The rector's wife has left him for another
man. He lives with his two daughters, his brother from the city, his
sister who keeps house for him and his old mother, 'the Mater',
who is the *de facto* head of the family. We are shown their mutual
torments in depth. Father is snarling and doggish, Uncle Fred is
stingy and grey-faced, Aunt Cissie has strange green flares of rage,
but the *pièce-de-résistance* is the Mater. She has the power of her

deformities. Her blindness means that she has to be led about. Her deafness allows her to dominate every conversation. She is like a malign queen bee, though she is also compared with an interloper toad that seeks to destroy the hive.

There are two young girls, daughters of the rector, and their lives are in process of being swallowed by this ménage. They have had their education abroad and do not feel the full weight of the rectory until they return home from school. They are physically quite unlike the other inhabitants of the rectory: tall, slender, fresh-faced. Yvette, in particular, has inherited her mother's temperament. She cannot adapt to the Sunday Schools, the Band of Hope and the Girls' Friendlies. Nor do motor excursions with the sons of local farmers attract her. But on one of these jaunts she is confronted with the gipsy.

Lawrence invests this figure with a glamour capable of acting as a counterbalance to the claustrophobic humours of the Rectory. Partly it is a matter of visualization – the gipsy is 'one of the black, loose-bodied handsome sort'. His gaze is 'insolent in its indifference'; his face 'swarthy and predative'. But the effect is cumulative: it builds up the suggestion of a dark presence beyond what was possible in the more simply naturalistic mode of 'The Daughters of the Vicar'. The image of the gipsy grows in the fertile imagination of the young girl. Whenever she thinks of him, it is as if his eyes are actually upon her, with the naked insinuation of desire. And with such psychic energy is associated a greater degree of alertness than the common run of men, a superior dexterity. Nearly all the tale is taken up with creating this contrast in atmospheres, between the rectory and what it stands for, and the gipsy.

There is a kind of sub-plot concerning a couple living together without benefit of clergy. They seem, on the face of it, ill-matched: a middle-ageing divorcée, and a youngish wastrel, very much ex-army. Yet they seem happy. '"What is it,"' wonders Yvette, '"that brings people together?"' Some hidden part of herself, which on the surface she has denied, has responded and still responds to the gipsy.

Even so, it takes a sudden action, the only genuinely external event in the tale, to precipitate contact between the virgin and the gipsy. An old gipsy, the gipsy grandmother, has told Yvette's fortune: '"Be braver in your body . . . Listen for the voice of water."' But the river swells into an uncanny mass, and suddenly a flood bursts down upon the rectory. An ancient tunnel, they discover later, has collapsed beneath the reservoir and brought down the dam. It is as though a primitive past has struck back at a decadent present. The flood is created with Lawrence's immense powers of description – 'a shaggy, tawny wave-front of water advancing like a wall of lions.' The house is struck again and again; the timbers begin to split. The gipsy, also caught in the flood, seizes Yvette and drags her through the flood to the upper floor and back chimney. This, he feels, will stand. As in 'The Princess' the couple clasp each other against the shuddering cold. But, unlike the Princess, the warmth of bodily contact proves to be Yvette's salvation. No sexual congress takes place – hence the title – but the affinity between Yvette and the gipsy is deep enough to dissolve the repressions of the rectory. The affinity is pre-conscious and animal. Not till the end of the tale does she realize that the gipsy has a name. Moreover, he is more than a figure of literal naturalism. He is associated with primitive force and the purgation of the flood. Indeed, everyone is altered for the better – even Aunt Cissie weeps with relief when Yvette is saved – with one exception. Significantly and symbolically, the oppressive Mater is drowned.

It can be seen, then, that there are themes in common among these eight tales. But they come to different conclusions. Daphne in 'The Ladybird' finds an affinity with the dark powers of the Count; but fulfilment lies beyond the grave. March is transmuted into femininity in 'The Fox', though her future remains uncertain in an imperfectly foreshadowed Canada. Louisa, in 'Daughters of the Vicar', marries her young miner, though she, too, has to live across the seas. Hannele in 'The Captain's Doll' achieves a relationship more alert and critical than that which is sought by the younger women in Lawrence's tales. The heroines of 'The Woman Who Rode Away' and 'St Mawr' transcend their sexuality; the heroine of 'The Princess' is destroyed by sex. And, as we have just seen, Yvette in 'The Virgin and the Gipsy' is purged of her antecedents by fire and flood. This shows how impossible it is to

NO ?

derive a philosophy from Lawrence's work. The eight tales precipitate themselves through observed particulars. Essentially they are the rendering of experience in evocative verbal terms. However, it does not seem to me that the last tale Lawrence was to write measures up to these qualities in its predecessors.

'The Escaped Cock' or 'The Man Who Died' (1927, 1928) – Lawrence preferred the earlier of these alternative titles – begins crisply:

There was a peasant near Jerusalem who acquired a young gamecock which looked a shabby little thing, but which put on brave feathers as spring advanced, and was resplendent with arched and orange neck by the time the fig trees were letting out leaves from their end-tips . . . 'He will surely fly away one of these days,' said the peasant's wife. So . . . they tied a cord round his shank, fastening it against the spur; and they tied the other end of the cord to the post that held up the donkey's straw pent-roof . . . One morning, just before the light of dawn, rousing from his slumbers with a sudden wave of strength, he leaped forward on his wings, and the string snapped . . .

He crows and awakens the peasant, who chases after him. Seeing a stranger in his way the peasant calls, '"O, stop him, master . . .! My escaped cock!"'

The stranger thus addressed is himself an escaped cock and also a man who has died. His coming back into consciousness, cold and sick, is done with physical immediacy and with deep empathy. But as we come to recognize this stranger as Jesus, the prose becomes, not so much portentous, as stylized. It is the early naturalistic details that speak to us. The Whitmanesque and quasi-Biblical diction – the two modes are by no means mutually exclusive – sets matters at a distance and renders them gnomic. '"Yet I would embrace multitudes, I who have never truly embraced even one. But Judas and the high priests saved me from my own salvation, and soon I can turn to my destiny like a bather in the sea at dawn, who has just come down to the shore alone."'

The opposed roles of the Mater and Joe Boswell in 'The Virgin and the Gipsy' are obviously symbolic, but they could not be so effective if they did not project and appeal on the literal level. It is the literal level that, after the splendid beginning, seems thin in 'The Escaped Cock'. In this later tale the risen Christ and the

Priestess of Isis make love; but the union does not have the symbolic force it ought to have. This is because the allegory is too little reinforced by the particularities of the event. Such a thinness is unusual enough in Lawrence's shorter fiction to deserve remark, though there are related failures in some of the novels and in much of the conceptual prose. It is a plot which is not in itself a fortunate one. We are taken too near the writings of George Moore and Oscar Wilde; we are reminded of Lawrence's less beneficial antecedents.

But certainly the best of the tales stand beside Melville's 'Benito Cereno', James's 'The Lesson of the Master' and Conrad's 'The Shadow Line' as superb examples of a form more appreciated than analysed. Essentially the affinities are with such works as Wordsworth's 'Michael' or Crabbe's 'Resentment'. Like these, Lawrence's tales concentrate on a restricted group of people. They sacrifice amplitude to economy; a sacrifice which is well worth making in the interests of focus. Lawrence is one of the supreme masters of this form. In it, he allies himself with the English narrative poets. However, I doubt whether in this prose semblance he has had significant successors. The true affinity of Lawrence's tales is with his last great stories, 'The Man Who Loved Islands' and 'Sun'; and with the finest of the Last Poems.

8 Stories (1924–29)

The Woman Who Rode Away (1928); *The Lovely Lady*
(1933)

Some of the late stories have in common a disbelief in humanity.
They tend to be terse; using little by way of context in order to
convey their basic theme. To this extent they are associated. But
there is, within this loose association, a group of stories which
interconnect quite closely. They share, rather oddly, a reliance
upon supernatural effect. They also share, even more oddly, the
expression of the author's hatred for certain former friends,
notably John Middleton Murry. Nevertheless, one or two stories
in this group have had considerable currency.

'The Rocking Horse Winner' (1926) was for many years one of
Lawrence's best-known works. It tells of a little boy who rides
himself to death on his rocking-horse in order to gain tips, from
that dubious agency, for the major horse-races. The story would
be hardly worth mentioning were it not powered by Lawrence's
hatred of money and the bourgeois life respectable. It never
transcends the linguistic limits of those same bourgeois characters
who say things like 'Right as a trivet!' and 'Poor devil!' – the
smallest of small-change in commonplace post-war conversation.
'Glad Ghosts' (1925) is equally crude in its means. At a country
house party there is an exchange of partners in some way, not
clearly specified, effected by the family ghost. And in some way
not defined the lady of the house bears a child fathered by the
Lawrentian narrator. The story begins, promisingly, with a
take-off of Lawrence's friend Dorothy Brett; but it continues dis-
appointingly, drawing for further traits of character and circumstance upon another friend, Lady Cynthia Asquith. Brett's characteristic deafness is settled upon the narrator, and this helps the
aura of mystery that pervades the story. But, in spite of this, the

whole amounts to little more than a ruinous adaptation of experience better handled in 'The Thimble' and 'The Ladybird'.

'The Last Laugh' (1924) also begins promisingly, with laughter on a snowy night in Hampstead:

the garden door of a tall, dark Georgian house suddenly opened, and three people confusedly emerged. A girl in a dark blue coat and fur turban, very erect: a fellow with a little dispatch-case, slouching: a thin man with a red beard, bareheaded, peering out of the gateway down the hill that swung in a curve downwards towards London.

'Look at it! A new world!' cried the man in the beard, ironically, as he stood on the step and peered out.

'No, Lorenzo! It's only whitewash!' cried the young man in the overcoat . . .

The man with the red beard is a Lawrentian *alter ego*, and he implicitly presides over the story, though this is his only explicit appearance. The girl is Brett again; her deafness is emphasized throughout. The man with the briefcase is Murry, and this makes the story one of several designed to bring about Murry's discomfiture. He enters the house of a dubious woman while the Brett-figure proceeds home under the protection of a young policeman who has come up to them in the night. There are various intimations that are evidently intended to convey the presence of Pan: a lit-up church, a figure glimpsed among the bushes, a puff of spring wind, extraordinary laughter. In the morning the policeman – who has been too frightened to leave the Brett-figure's house – is found to have grown a club foot like the weird paw of some animal. While the Murry figure, who has returned 'furtive' and 'shambling', collapses and dies, presumably at the sight of Pan, with 'the horrible grin of a man who realizes he has made a . . . fatal fool of himself'. This is the kind of material E. M. Forster could have managed far better than Lawrence. Whimsy has no place in Lawrence's temperament. In any case, the story is flawed by the unassimilated animus towards Murry.

This flows into the ridiculous in 'The Border Line' (1924, 1928). Murry here is caricatured as a knowing little Highlander who marries the widow (a Frieda figure) of his friend, a Lawrence expanded into a red-haired fighting Celt. But the Celt comes back from the grave and seizes the woman, whereupon the Murry-figure is made to die in this story, too, and 'on his face was a sickly grin of a thief caught in the very act'. Even if the reader were unaware of the biographical sources of the story, such unbacked violence of diction as this would alert him to its hollowness and lack of motivation.

This *leitmotiv* of the rictus occurs also in 'Smile' (1925). When the Murry-figure's wife expires in a hospice (Katherine Mansfield died in the Gurdjieff Institute in Fontainebleau) her husband cannot resist an involuntary smile. But the smile passes from him to the corpse and then – 'never was man more utterly smileless'.

Yet the author who wrote this used something of the same material in 'Jimmy and the Desperate Woman' (1924). The difference is that this latter story is far lighter and more deft in touch. It is not so much allegory or symbolic drama as comedy – dark comedy, it is true, but a mode far more suitable for shaping negation and animus into a story with a point.

It is largely a matter of putting the Murry-figure – here called Jimmy – into perspective; seeing, in fact, the funny side. Far more social context is given to him here than in the other stories – a divorce, the editorship of a highbrow magazine. The presentation, too, is more interestingly complex. There is a gap between Jimmy's opinion of himself as a hard-done-by Saint Sebastian and the way in which he appears to his male friends – as a consistently grinning faun. His female friends see him as a fascinating little man with the capacity to make a woman feel like a queen.

They are only picking up Jimmy's own illusion about women. After his divorce he wants someone who will submit – a Ruth, a Gretchen, a Tess of the D'Urbervilles. So when a couple of poems for his magazine come from a coal-miner's wife who lives in the Industrial North, Jimmy tries to make this woman fit the crudely fashioned archetype in his mind.

It is Jimmy that is crude, however, not the story. The description of the sophisticated little man wading through icy black mud to Mrs Pinnegar's dark and remote street is as acutely comic as anything Lawrence penned. 'His skin crept a little. The place felt uncanny and hostile, hard, as if iron and minerals breathed into the black air.' A good many visitors from the Home Counties have been thus affected by the Industrial North! And Mrs Pinnegar proves to be as bleak as her surroundings: a woman stranded on the reefs. She is at loggerheads with her husband, who has another woman, and she hates the place where she lives. Jimmy feels uneasy and challenged and, on impulse, makes his dramatic gesture: '"Why don't you come and live with me?" he said, like the little gambler he was.'

Once home, he has to face the jeers of his friends, and his own sinking feeling. A letter designed to put her off has no effect: this really is a desperate woman. His intervention may be a gesture to Jimmy, but for Mrs Pinnegar it is a door to a new life. We finish the story feeling the aura of an impossible situation. How is the sickly, excitable Jimmy to live with the inexorable, smouldering Emilia? The story is told with something of the terse vivacity one associates with the earlier chapters of *The Lost Girl*. And, although the end of the affair is not in doubt, still there is enough material there for a novel, and a remarkable novel at that.

Many of the stories, and not only the ones aimed at Murry, are spoiled by rancour unabsorbed into any narrative framework. 'Rawdon's Roof' (1927, 1928) is the debunking of a misogynist whose claim is that no woman sleeps under his roof; but the central character is not worth the trouble Lawrence takes to debunk him. 'The Overtone' (1924) is largely a middle-aged man's meditation about the way in which his wife rejected him in youth. 'The Blue Moccasins' (1928) also shows a disaffected couple. Matters rise to a head when the moccasins of the title, a gift from the elderly wife to her middle-ageing husband, are used as props for amateur theatricals in the village schoolroom. 'The Lovely Lady' (1927), too, is preoccupied with objects: the heroine uses them to keep a hold over her son and her niece. A clumsy device – the niece overhears a soliloquy – leads to recognition of the well-preserved lady's true character; she grows suddenly old, and dies. There is bitterness in all these stories; but at what trivia it is directed!

'Things' (1927) is equally bitter but makes more interesting use of its properties. The trivialities here are not possessions of the story but of its characters. Indeed, their belongings are the determining factors of their lives: Louis Quinze side-tables, a Venetian book-case, above all, 'curtains of queer ancient material that looked like finely-knitted silk . . . Valerie hardly ever came

into the *salotto* without mentally falling on her knees before the
curtains . . .'. To her they are Chartres, and this is the theme of the
story; hardly a trivial one. It is the mistaking of *objets d'art* for a
way of life. The 'things' of the story are not, in any real sense,
used, and yet they represent, for their owners, life and culture.
The lives of these owners are drained of meaning: they are
dilettantes with no work in the world. And when, eventually,
economic circumstances force them to return to their native
America so that the husband can take a job, the final irony is that
he does so primarily to support the Bologna cupboard, the
Ravenna chair, the Chartres curtains – the 'things', in fact. The
cultural idealism of the Melvilles is shown to be the crudest
materialism of the tourist, collector or entrepreneur. It is faithfully
reflected in their final dialogue.

'Europe's the mayonnaise all right, but America supplies the good old
lobster – what?'
'Every time!' she said, with satisfaction.

Things, too, assert themselves in one of the finest of these late
stories, 'Mother and Daughter' (1928). It is a reduced and
embittered 'St Mawr', without the horses. Like Mrs Witt, Mrs
Bodoin is a destructive weapon who demoralizes the men who, on
the surface, she wishes would court her somewhat marasmic
daughter. She has set up a flat for the purpose, and prominent
among its painted cabinets and brocade chairs is an Aubusson
carpet. So detached is Mrs Bodoin from the business of living that
she dubs the only suitor that presents himself a carpet salesman;
and she means it as an insult. But this gentleman, an elderly
Armenian, sits in masculine calm behind what appears to be an
oriental submissiveness. This masculinity brings out the harem
spirit in the wan Virginia. Equally in character, it defeats Mrs
Bodoin, who retreats from the Aubusson carpet and its environs
to eke out her days in Paris. The elderly Armenian is left in
possession: from 'Mother and Daughter' we have moved, in an
adapted way, to 'Father and Daughter'.
    No materialist himself, Lawrence understood materialism. But
it was hard for him to avoid reducing it to a scheme, as in the story

called 'Two Blue Birds' (1926). These blue birds fight for dominance under the feet of a successful novelist while he dictates narcissistic rubbish to his humble secretary. The ménage is held up to ironic contemplation, ostensibly through the eyes of the novelist's estranged and wolfish wife. But her view is too near that of Lawrence himself; indeed, all too often, explicitly he takes over her role. And the device of the blue birds is too externally used. Once more, one feels, animus has encroached upon technique.

The concept of materialism was one that Lawrence hacked and hacked at in these later stories. It is true that 'The Man who was Through with the World' (1927) may have been intended to show that no man is independent of human society, even though he be a hermit. But in many ways this theme ran counter to Lawrence's predilections in this period and so the story remains unfinished.

On the other hand 'The Man Who Loved Islands' (1926) is one of Lawrence's masterpieces, and is all the richer for building up the narcissistic character portrayed in 'Two Blue Birds' and giving him more of a context. This central character dabbles in writing, is a dandy in appearance and an amateur, too, of husbandry. He cannot bear the mainland and tries to create a self-sufficient world on an island: the effort nearly ruins him financially.

There is a special tone in which the Master's love of islands is described. He wants to fill an island with his own personality; he wants it to be a nest to hold one egg, the Islander himself; cosy, homelike, the perfect place, all filled with his own blossom-like spirit. In other words, an island ought to be a simulacrum of the womb. When the original island fails to measure up, or down, to that idea, he moves to a smaller one. He takes, however, a skeleton staff.

This, perhaps, is his trouble. The next island is a hump of rock in the sea, and contains only a small house and two cottages joined together. But in one of them lives a widow and her daughter who helps in the house. The daughter, a more naturalistic aspect of the novelist's secretary in 'Two Blue Birds', even helps with his work. So naturally she helps in other ways, too, and becomes pregnant with the Master's child. Appalled by this intrusion of society, he leaves her and seeks out a third island.

Here he can certainly be by himself. This island is virtually inaccessible because of the difficult seas. There are no inhabitants, only the seabirds and a few sheep, and he soon gets rid of the latter. The result is a slow recession, done in imagery redolent of the womb. His mind turns soft and hazy like the ocean; he sees mirages of other islands, but they are quite without substance; he wants to hear nothing but the great silence; all interest leaves him; the world has grown eerie; he derives his satisfaction from being alone.

As he atrophies, his 'world' diminishes. Even the seabirds fly away. The snow falls, he becomes ill, the sky darkens, there is the threat of more snow. He has so far slackened his hold on life that life has slackened its hold on him.

The story is superbly told. Each island is an entity, with a character of its own. The supporting characters – the human ones – are deftly touched in. And the central character stands aloof, in his way as recognizable and untouchable as Egbert in 'England, my England'. His fear of life is enshrouded in vagueness, dilettantism; his love of islands is a progressive retreat. This, together with 'Sun' which was originally written the year before, seems to me the crucial story of Lawrence's last phase.

Until recently 'Sun' (1925, 1928) was accessible only in a private edition except in a short form. This gave a truncated idea of a remarkable story.

The basic datum of both versions is a city woman seeking out the sun. She separates temporarily from her husband, a New York businessman, and sails with her small boy to what appears, from internal evidence, to be Sicily. The plot is simple. Juliet lies in the sun and browns and ripens until her husband, somewhat reluctantly, joins her. There is, however, a significant difference between the versions. In the short text the sun appears naturalistically as a force bringing Juliet to fruition. In the long version there is a further dimension: the sun is a lover and is described in a series of images, which do not occur in the short text, that fuse together a fierce sun-worship and a violent sensuality:

he was full and naked. And she wanted to come to him . . .

. . . exulting that at last it was no human lover . . .

. . . Only her womb remained tense and resistant, the eternal resistance. It would resist even the sun . . .

. . . And she felt again the unyielding resistance of her womb, against him and everything . . .

. . . And her tense womb, though still closed, was slowly unfolding, slowly, slowly, like a lily bud under water, as the sun mysteriously touched it . . .

. . . The true Juliet lived in the dark flow of the sun within her deep body, like a river of dark rays circling, circling dark and violet round the sweet, shut bud of her womb . . .

. . . Her womb was coming open wide with rosy ecstasy, like a lotus flower . . .

These quotations indicate a gradual development in the story. They do not occur in the short version and so the story in that form seems more static than in fact it is. And the symbolic aura, the sun as fructifier, is considerably reduced. In its shorter form, indeed, the story appears to be little more than a paean in favour of sunbathing. But the last quotation in particular comes from a passage which is crucial. It shows clearly that Juliet's resistance to the sun has been overcome and she is, for the first time in her life, open to love.

Hard upon this revelation comes an episode not in any real sense given to us in the expurgated version. One day Juliet is, as usual, walking naked from her sunbathing back to her house, when she encounters a peasant.

The encounter has, in the longer version, a powerful physicality:

Still they looked into each other's eyes, and the fire flowed between them, like the blue streaming fire from the heart of the sun. And she saw the phallus rise under his clothing . . .

The use of the word 'phallus' helps to give the passage an archetypal quality. In association with phrases like 'blue streaming fire' and 'the heart of the sun' it makes the peasant the mortal embodiment of the mystical ripening hitherto associated with Juliet's halcyon days. But in the shorter version this encounter is put at the end of the story, in retrospect – 'Once, in the hot morning . . . she had come upon him . . .' It is also less powerful. Instead of the monumental phrasing of the longer version we have virtual clichés – 'a flame . . . melting her bones', for example. The peasant is introduced separately, as a figure seen at a distance across the gully. This comes after the husband's reappearance in the shorter version of the story. The intensity of the encounter is in this version dispersed, and the peasant's relationship with the sun is lost in the process.

My comparison is a way of indicating the innate power of the longer text. The comparison would hold valid even if it were proved, as some have surmised, that it is the shorter version that is the original. Either way the story requires a fuller compass to give it scope. It is a hymn to the sun; a celebration of the body; and a fusion of both into a display of uninhibited sexuality. 'Sun' is none the less positive for beginning and ending with the city existence which Juliet is seeking to escape. That existence is described as a machine, as a fixed wheel of circumstance, and, in its turn, is identified with the hostile atmosphere of Juliet's marriage.

Nothing is more extraordinary in Lawrence's later work than the power with which life is evoked through the perception of his imminent dissolution. Towards the end, Lawrence became interested in what would now be called science fiction. In his hands, however, it assumes a mythic quality seldom found in the genre. Keith Sagar, who republished the unexpurgated 'Sun', renamed the editorially titled 'Autobiographical Fragment' (1927) more aptly 'A Dream of Life'. It takes off from William Morris's *News from Nowhere*, in that a man goes to sleep in this world and wakes up in an ideal world of the future. But the present is visualized with a power that, in his fictional as distinct from his conceptual work, Morris could never have commanded – 'the mean houses shabby and scaly', 'the pit fuming silently'. And the awakening into the future is redolent of the ecstatic landscape of 'The Woman Who Rode Away', not so much in descriptive particularity, but in feeling and tone of description:

So as they washed me, I came to myself. I even sat up. And I saw earth and rock, and a sky that I knew was afternoon. And I was stark-naked, and there were two men washing me, and they too were stark-naked. But I was white, pure white, and thin, and they were ruddy, and not thin . . .

The ugly colliery townlet of dirty red bricks is no longer there. Instead, 'a town, all yellow in the late afternoon light, with yellow,

curved walls rising massive from the yellow-leaved orchards . . .'
This sense of reawakening is carried on in a dialogue whose
imagery foreshadows that of 'The Ship of Death', one of Lawrence's last poems: 'You went to sleep, like a chrysalis: in one of
the earth's little chrysalis wombs . . . and you woke up like a
butterfly . . .'

The story seems to be unfinished, but it says what it has to say –
that people need not live mechanically and in squalor, that vision
and co-operation could make this world a paradise. The fault of the
story is not that it ends too soon; it is rather that its first thirty-one
paragraphs form a short essay, detachable from the story as a
whole. In other words, the story *begins* too soon. The proper start
would be at the paragraph beginning, with a master's touch, 'It is a
soft, hazy October day . . .'

Another story in the same genre, also technically unfinished, is
'The Undying Man' (1927). It does not have the quality of
concreteness manifest in 'A Dream of Life'. Instead, in execution
it is more like certain aspects of 'The Escaped Cock'. But it
possesses a terseness denied to that somewhat overrated tale and
suited to the parable which it really is. Two learned men, the Jew
Maimonides and the Christian Aristotle, find out that they can
make a homunculus by cutting a vein from a living man and
growing it among certain herbs in a glass jar. The drawback is that
the man from whom the vein is cut will die; the advantage is that
the homunculus will live for ever. Aristotle is chosen by lot to make
the sacrifice, and he asks his friend in no way to impede the growth
of the creature that will result from his death. The agonies of
Maimonides as he watches the homunculus grow are powerfully
projected – he sees 'that strange red light, like no light of God,
which glowed so tiny and yet was so fierce and strong'. Clearly a
horrible blasphemy has been perpetrated. Yet Maimonides has
sworn to his friend that he will not destroy it. The text here breaks
off, but S. S. Koteliansky published the Yiddish original, from
which Lawrence had taken the story, in translation in *The London
Mercury* for February 1937. It is quoted by Dr Sagar in his edition
of Lawrence's later short stories, published under the title of *The
Princess*. One can read from the end of the story as it is now
straight on to Koteliansky, and this allows for a reasonable, if not

wholly satisfying, conclusion. Maimonides tells the servants to let the household fowls into the room where the jar containing the homunculus stands. He prays, as is his wont, marching up and down, and his flapping cloak so scares the fowls that they fly about and one upsets the jar which breaks in pieces. 'And when Maimonides saw that the tiny little creature pointed a tiny little finger to him as a sign that he had broken his oath to Aristotle, Maimonides wept bitterly, and all the rest of his life prayed for forgiveness.'

In this last period of Lawrence's fiction-writing, then, we see four distinct groups of stories. The least valuable are those of 1924–26 which link up Murry with various supernatural occasions. They are bitter in tone and negative in content and are only kept from total mediocrity by occasional flashes, mostly occurring by way of introduction, and by the redeemingly comic 'Jimmy and the Desperate Woman'. The central sector consists of some eight stories (1924, 1926–29), where bitterness is rendered more realistically. These are, on the whole, not Lawrence at his best. There are exceptions to this in 'Things' and 'Mother and Daughter' which show successfully, as the other stories do not, people atrophied by material possessions. The only two really great stories of the period stand apart: 'The Man Who Loved Islands' (1926) and 'Sun' (1925, 1928). These show some apprehension of a negative civilization but are irradiated with an enlivening sense of more positive qualities. Finally the two science fiction stories of 1927 show Lawrence refusing to be bound by the predilections even of his own earlier work. In their elegiac beauty they look forward to the Last Poems; and both suggest that even in the teeth of impending death Lawrence was attempting to survey still more remote horizons.

9 Poems (1920–29)

Birds, Beasts and Flowers (1923); *Pansies* (1929);
Nettles (1930); *Last Poems* (1932); *Fire* (1940)

By 1914, the sequence *Look! We Have Come Through!* was
nearing its end. Lawrence was to write more of the sequence, up to
'Craving for Spring' (February 1917), but the basic impulse was
spent with 'History' (July 1913), its last distinguished piece. The
final poems written between 1915 and 1917 ('"She Said As Well
To Me"', 'New Heaven and Earth', 'Manifesto') are Whitmanesque without the qualities of Whitman.

Between 1914 and 1920 Lawrence wrote comparatively few
poems. These were years of Lawrence's enforced residence in
England, acute poverty, and his concentration upon the greatest
of his novels. What verse there was consisted in part of war poems
adapted from the translations out of Arabic and into German
made by his uncle-in-law, Fritz Krenkow. And it was, coin-
cidentally, to Krenkow that Lawrence wrote one of his earliest
letters in praise of Sicily (20 March 1920). Here, as if in celebration
of the landscape he fell in love with – its green wheat, olives and
almond trees – Lawrence produced between May 1920 and
September 1921 the bulk of *Birds, Beasts and Flowers*.

This seems to be Lawrence's most deliberately composed book
of poems. That is to say that the poems stand in relation one to
another, rather than streaming along like the fortuitous plasm of a
diary. As in the better poems of *Look! We Have Come Through!*
Lawrence is strongest when he ceases to regard himself and
observes instead some extraneous object. A quick sympathy for
living things can be seen in the earliest of his works, in 'Campions'
and 'Guelder Roses', 'The Wild Common' or 'Baby Running
Barefoot'; and this is to say nothing of such short stories as 'Goose
Fair', 'A Lesson on a Tortoise' and 'The Old Adam'. The insights

manifested in such pieces as these developed into the artist's vision of *Birds, Beasts and Flowers.*

The first of these poems to be written was 'Mosquito' (May 1920). This creature, which anybody else might dismiss as a nuisance, Lawrence contemplates with wry interest:

> When did you start your tricks
> Monsieur?
>
> What do you stand on such high legs for?
> Why this length of shredded shank
> You exaltation?

But it was in 'Snake', one of the finest poems of the sequence, that Lawrence came into his own (July 1920). Here we have the slow, cadenced setting of atmosphere, even down to a deliberate dislocation of syntax.

> A snake came to my water-trough
> On a hot, hot day, and I in pyjamas for the heat,
> To drink there . . .

We have the almost incomparable Lawrentian eye for natural detail:

> He reached down from a fissure in the earth-wall in the gloom
> And trailed his yellow-brown slackness soft-bellied down,
>   over the edge of the stone trough . . .

The poet himself is present, but present as an adjunct. In contrast with the integrity of the snake, the human being is at odds with himself. The voices of his education make war upon his instinctive empathy with the snake:

> And voices in me said, If you were a man
> You would take a stick and break him now, and finish him off.
>
> But must I confess how I liked him,
> How glad I was he had come like a guest in quiet, to drink
>   at my water-trough . . .

As with all the finer poems of *Birds, Beasts and Flowers*, the natural description is synergic – amounting to more than the sum of its parts. It brings into question what a man is – the set super-ego that triumphs:

> I looked round, I put down my pitcher,
> I picked up a clumsy log
> And threw it at the water-trough with a clatter . . .

The snake convulses in haste – the poet's loss of dignity in throwing the log is a violation of nature – and disappears. The poet himself is left to write the poem in tones of elegiac regret as an expiation for missing a chance – in Lawrence's memorable phrase – with one of 'the lords of life'.

This is a wonderful description of a snake. It is also a short story as firm as any of Lawrence's minor masterpieces in that genre. 'Snake' is a disquisition upon the failure of man to take an appropriate place in the physical universe.

The early autumn of 1920 was one of the creative moments of Lawrence's life. It followed hard upon the composition of 'Snake' with a sequence within the sequence: 'Tortoises'. This, as Keith Sagar suggests, is really one long poem in six sections. The marvellous eye is everywhere present: 'A tiny, fragile, half-animate bean . . .' ('Baby Tortoise'); 'Stepping, wee mite, in his loose trousers . . .' ('Tortoise-Shell'); '. . . all rambling aimless, like little perambulating pebbles scattered in the garden . . .' ('Tortoise Family Connections'). There is a sustaining wit:

> It is no use my saying to him in an emotional voice:
> 'This is your Mother, she laid you when you were an egg.'
>
> He does not even trouble to answer: 'Woman, what have I
>   to do with thee?'
> He wearily looks the other way
> And she even more wearily looks another way still . . .
>
> ('Tortoise Family Connections')

The mother tortoise is seen as a recognizable character: large, matronly and sardonic – as if domesticity had driven her to cynicism. Recognizable, too, is the father tortoise scuffling beside her like an importunate old man (see 'Lui et Elle'). Lawrence operates an eclectic range of anthropomorphic device in order to project the various identities of these tortoises. It is, in the upshot, a comedy of sexuality –

> I heard a woman pitying her, pitying the Mère Tortue.
> While I, I pity Monsieur.
> 'He pesters her and torments her,' said the woman.
> How much more is *he* pestered and tormented, say I . . . ('Lui et Elle')

The whole poem explodes into an orgiastic revelation in 'Tortoise Shout' where the tortoise shrieks in coition:

> giving that fragile yell, that scream,
> Super-audible,
> From his pink, cleft, old-man's mouth,
> Giving up the ghost,
> Or screaming in Pentecost, receiving the ghost . . .

Then, in a tremendous series of similes, Lawrence links bird, beast and human being in a concatenation of relationships turning upon the impulse of sex common to us all – the scream of a frog, the cry of wild geese, the scream of a rabbit, the blorting of a heifer in heat, the howl of cats, the sound of a woman in labour, the bleat of a lamb, the wail of an infant, the passionate tenor of a collier long since dead:

> Sex, which breaks us into voice, sets us calling across
>   the deeps, calling, calling for the complement,
> Singing, and calling, and singing again, being answered,
>   having found.
> Torn, to become whole again, after long seeking for
>   what is lost,
> The same cry from the tortoise as from Christ, the
>   Osiris-cry of abandonment,
> That which is whole, torn asunder,
> That which is in part, finding its whole again throughout
>   the universe.

The Tortoise poem is Lawrence's central statement in *Birds, Beasts and Flowers*. It is a brilliant amalgam of natural description, comic characterization and apprehension of the life force which drives the world. It makes its effect, as 'Snake' does, cumulatively. Many of the techniques are prose techniques, and, it has to be admitted, the form is not the controlling pattern that it is, say, in

'Giorno dei Morti', that corner-stone of the earlier sequence, *Look! We Have Come Through!* But the complex of emotions and the unflagging energy of invention carry the poet along. 'Tortoises' is undoubtedly a central document in Lawrence's immense output.

Also in the early autumn of 1920, Lawrence celebrated the mythical past of the vegetable world in 'Grapes' – 'There was another world, a dusky, flowerless, tendrilled world/ . . . Of which world, the vine was the invisible rose . . .' This mythic past had already been invoked in a poem that prefigures the science fiction interests of our own day: 'Humming Bird' (June 1920) – 'We look at him through the wrong end of the long telescope of Time . . .' In these months, also, Lawrence produced his own favourite poem of the collection, 'Slag-wattled turkey-cock,/Dross-jabot' – a use of language vivacious and highly inventive. Lawrence was never more himself than at this time. But he was not certain how far to go on. He speaks in March 1921 of the book as being finished; but, of the Sicilian poems alone, were to come 'Fish', 'Bat' and 'Man and Bat' (September 1921) – 'It was the light of day which he could not enter,/Any more than I could enter the white-hot door of a blast furnace . . .' And, tiring of Sicily – 'a world of . . . *canaille, canaglia, Schweinhunderei*, stink-pots' – he accepted Mabel Dodge's offer of a house and set sail, taking the long way round, to Taos, in New Mexico. Ceylon gave Lawrence the poem 'Elephant' (March 1922), with its unforgettable portrait of a pale and dejected Prince of Wales. In Australia he found the Kangaroo and her imprisoned cub – 'a lean little face comes out, as from a window' (July 1922). And so on to New Mexico, and the last of the birds and beasts. Among others, these include 'The Red Wolf', 'The Blue Jay' and the immensely attractive 'Mountain Lion' (January 1923) – 'her bright striped frost-face will never watch any more, out of the shadow of the cave in the blood-orange rock'.

This line, may, however, give us a sense of what is missing from the book. Is it really verse? What would happen if we wrote 'Mountain Lion' out as prose?

Climbing through the January snow, into the Lobo canyon, dark grow the spruce trees, blue is the balsam, water sounds still unfrozen, and the trail is still evident.

Men! Two men! Men! The only animal in the world to fear!
They hesitate. We hesitate. They have a gun. We have no gun.
Then we all advance, to meet.
Two Mexicans, strangers, emerging out of the dark and snow and
inwardness of the Lobo valley. What are they doing here on this
vanishing trail?
What is he carrying? Something yellow. A deer?
'Qué tiene, amigo?'
'León – '

What is immediately noticeable is Lawrence's paragraphing – it
would injure the sense to disrupt it. There is, however, no kindred
inevitability as to the line-endings. The first paragraph is composed of two lines; the second of three; but no one could gather
that from the rhythm. One could, in other words, amalgamate the
'verse' lines. And yet it would be clumsy to run the two paragraphs
together. Moreover, the tone is astonishingly at one with the final
version of *Studies in Classic American Literature*, a near-
contemporary work, which also uses short paragraphs, exclama-
tions, vivacious imagery. This suggests that 'Mountain Lion'
belongs to a prose rather than to a verse tradition; and that is true
of a great number of Lawrence's poems. Even the more articulated 'Snake', 'Tortoises' and 'Turkey-Cock' are related in technique to the short stories rather than to any poems other than
Lawrence's own. Almost alone among poets, he seems to have
seen verse as his journal, an experiential plasm. In contrast, his
prose at its best, in the tales and the short stories, has the fineness
of structure we associate with operative form; where structure
does not merely go along with content, but mimetically and
graphically acts it out.

One can see the verse inoperatively loosening in these later
phases of *Birds, Beasts and Flowers*. The paragraphs have become
increasingly detached, one from another, in, for instance, 'Spirits
Summoned West' (October 1922); here, indeed, they turn almost
into separate poems. Further, there emerges, as in 'The American
Eagle' (March 1923), an impatient scolding tone. This tone
is based, all too frequently, on nothing more remarkable than
cliché – 'Are you the goose that lays the golden egg . . .?/That
addled golden egg?'. The form has broken down even further in a

group of poems, *Fire* (published posthumously, in 1940). The
following dates from April 1924:

Americans!
The word stands for something,
  carries its own patent, and its own obligation.

Americans are the people of America.
The destiny of America is in their hands.
The living America is in the hearts of Americans . . . ('O! Americans')

But there was little verse in the next six years. These were the
years of the greatest tales: 'The Captain's Doll' had already been
written in Sicily, but 'St Mawr' was written in New Mexico in 1924
and 'The Virgin and the Gipsy' soon after Lawrence's return to
Italy at the end of 1925. Little verse all this time; then there was an
eruption. The famous or infamous *Pansies*, anglicé *Pensées*, i.e.
'Thoughts', came towards the end of 1928. The initial cause seems
to have been a good deal of police interference with the novel of
that year, *Lady Chatterley's Lover*. A number of copies of the
privately printed first edition had been seized. Most of these
Pansies were blow-offs in response to this; hastily written and of
indifferent poetic merit. They were published in July 1929. Even
at this point, through police insistence, fourteen of the poems
were dropped. And, in the same month, the confiscation from the
Warren Gallery, London, of thirteen of Lawrence's paintings was
a further exacerbation. It gave rise to a sequence of even more
disagreeable poems, all dating from July and August 1929, called
Nettles. Lawrence continued to write 'Pansies' throughout 1929,
and a collection of no less than 205 was published, with other work
of greater moment, in *Last Poems* after his death. There are thirty-
four further Pansies which remained in holograph for years and
which were eventually published in the Pinto edition of the
Complete Poems. One of them is called 'So there!' In many ways,
that would do as a generic title for the entire sequence.

But, in fact, such a judgment would be unfair. There are
individual *Pansies* of great clarity, and between eleven and
twenty, according to where one sets one's sights, deserve a place
among Lawrence's classics. This is not many out of a total roll call
of some 690 pieces, but at least they place Lawrence with the

satirists. Of the seizure of his paintings Lawrence wrote, scathingly:

> Virginal, pure policemen came
> And hid their faces for very shame,
>
> while they carried the shameless things away
> to gaol, to be hid from the light of day.
>
> And Mr Mead, that old, old lily
> said: 'Gross! coarse! hideous!' and I, like a silly,
>
> thought he meant the faces of the police-court officials,
> and how right he was, and I signed my initials . . . ('Innocent England')

But this, in its relatively formal couplets, is an exception to the usual mode of *Pansies* and *Nettles* – a mode which could best be described as deliberately improvisatory.

Characteristic of *Pansies*, though better than the average run, is a piece marked by terseness of idea, deftness of language, the neat placing of an attitude which is in itself comic or absurd. It is called 'Ultimate Reality', and I quote it in full:

> A young man said to me:
> I am interested in the problem of reality.
>
> I said: Really!
> Then I saw him turn to glance again, surreptitiously,
> in the big mirror, at his own fascinating shadow.

That is about as effective as the *Pansies*, in their basic mode, get. But there is a limit to the amount of protest and admonition one can take, even when it is trenchantly expressed.

> There are no gods, and you can please yourself
> have a game of tennis, go out in the car, do some shopping,
>   sit and talk, talk, talk
> with a cigarette browning your fingers . . . ('There Are No Gods')

And this, in any case, would have carried more weight if linked with some show of mimetic expression – as happens, to some extent, in 'Bells':

> That hard clapper striking in a hard mouth
> and resounding after with a long hiss of insistence
> is obscene . . .

It follows that the more successful *Pansies* are those which have most sense of context.

There are, for instance, poems which look back to the *Birds, Beasts and Flowers* of 'Grapes' and 'Humming-Bird'. Consider 'Terra Incognita', especially in its lyrical final cadence:

> when at last we escape the barbed-wire enclosure
> of *Know Thyself*, knowing we can never know,
> we can but touch, and wonder, and ponder, and make our effort
> and dangle in a last fastidious fine delight
> as the fuchsia does, dangling her reckless drop
> of purple after so much putting forth
> and slow mounting marvel of a little tree.

Characteristically, the plant here celebrated by Lawrence is one of the most ancient species surviving. Amid the protestations of *Pansies*, the poet's eye has not dimmed. We find in 'Andraitx-Pomegranate Flowers', the result of a visit from Italy to Majorca in June 1929, this:

> Short gasps of flame in the green of night, way off
> the pomegranates are in flower,
> small sharp red fires in the night of leaves . . .

Such imagistic vitality is occasionally conjoined – especially in *More Pansies*, the collection that appeared with *Last Poems* – with a sombre wisdom that irradiates the best of those later pieces. Consider 'The Hostile Sun':

> Sometimes the sun turns hostile to men
> when the daytime consciousness has got overweening
> when thoughts are stiff, like old leaves
> and ideas are hard, like acorns ready to fall . . .

What interfuses this is not the acerbity of the *Pansies* proper but the premonition of approaching death. It is this that characterizes the better poems in the series and allows them a fugitive lyricism. This is seen in a poem I quote complete, 'Desire is Dead':

> Desire may be dead
> and still a man can be
> a meeting place for sun and rain,

> wonder outwaiting pain
> as in a wintry tree.

Thought works in this poem: witness the idea that the capacity of wonder in man can survive the death-pangs of desire. One must admire, as well, the way in which the author leads up to that final image of the wintry tree; the man, as well as the tree, is outwardly dead and nevertheless still can be a meeting-place. The rhymes, too, are a pattern of the sense; only the first is a dead end. The formal linking of the others is an indication of growth and contact. The poem, small as it seems, is a masterpiece of form.

The best *Pansies*, it appears, are those which are least character-istic of the collection as a whole. They are those poems which look back to *Birds, Beasts and Flowers* or, better still, which prefigure the imaginings of the *Last Poems*: 'Fatality' ('the dark Hades at the roots of the tree'); 'Trees in the Garden' ('they stand so still/in the thunder air, all strangers to one another'); and 'Flowers and Men', a fine answer to those who accuse Lawrence of mindless primitivism:

> Oh leave off saying I want you to be savages.
> Tell me, is the gentian savage, at the top of its coarse stem?
> Oh what in you can answer to this blueness?
>
> I want you to be as savage as the gentian and the daffodil.
> Tell me! tell me! is there in you a beauty to compare
> to the honeysuckle at evening now
> pouring out the breath of his godhead.

This is spiritually part of *Last Poems* (autumn, 1929) where Lawrence's poetic powers were extended to their farthest reach.

In one's recollection, all the *Last Poems* tend to be coloured by their greatest achievements. They seem like a song-cycle tem-pered to the pitch and quality of the deepest voice, the *basso profondo*, descending lower and lower to the ultimate C. But in fact there is a good deal of energy and bite in these poems. This is so even though Lawrence was fatally ill, in Bavaria and the South of France, when he wrote them. There is, in no bad sense, a carry-over from the more positive of the *Pansies*. Consider 'The Greeks are Coming'; 'Red Geranium and Godly Mignonette' ('even God could not imagine the redness of a red geranium'); and 'Demiurge':

> as if any Mind could have imagined a lobster
> dozing in the under-deeps, then reaching out a savage
>   and iron claw . . .!

It is questionable how far many of these *Last Poems* are separate one from another. Interdependence is obvious in the last two quotations. Nevertheless there are some poems articulated enough to stand by themselves. One thinks, in the Homeric 'Man of Tyre', of the lyrical yearning for a beautiful girl wading in the water –

> Oh lovely, lovely with the dark hair piled up, as she
>   went deeper, deeper down the channel, then rose
>   shallower, shallower,
> with the full thighs slowly lifting of the wader wading
>   shorewards
> and the shoulders pallid with light from the silent sky behind . . .

Yet this poem, self-sufficient though it is, relates to other poems about the sea: 'They Say the Sea is Loveless', 'Whales Weep Not!' 'Mana of the Sea'. And these, in their turn, relate to one of the most secure of Lawrence's masterpieces, 'The Ship of Death'.

Critics have suggested that this poem is not wholly finished. Richard Aldington, an early editor, said that Lawrence meant eventually to combine all the poems from 'The Ship of Death' to 'Phoenix' at the end of the manuscript into one whole. This seems doubtful. Rather, in composition, smaller poems bud off from the main trunk of 'The Ship of Death' and are culled to form the later pieces. A whole area of 'The Ship of Death' in draft is devoted to a meditation upon those dead who cannot set sail because they are not prepared to die:

> Oh pity the dead that are dead, but cannot take
> the journey, still they moan and beat
> against the silvery adamant walls of this our exclusive
>   existence . . .

Or again:

> Pity, oh pity the poor dead that are only ousted from life
> and crowd there on the grey mud beaches of the margins,
> gaunt and horrible . . .

There is no equivalent for this in the final version of 'The Ship of Death'. Instead the idea was taken up and rehandled in separate, though related, poems.

> Oh pity the dead that are dead, but cannot take
> the journey, still they moan and beat
> against the silvery adamant walls of life's exclusive city . . .
>
> ('The Houseless Dead')

> . . . Oh, now as November draws near
> the grey, grey reaches of earth's shadow,
> the long, mean marginal stretches of our existence
> are crowded with lost souls, the uneasy dead . . .
>
> ('Beware the Unhappy Dead')

Instead of brooding on the dead who are left behind, 'The Ship of Death', pruned of such negative ideas, moves into a sustained meditation upon the soul who will take the journey. It is a bruised soul, a shrinking soul, that embarks; and for this reason Lawrence abandoned in draft a further idea, that of the soul wrapped in its dark-red mantle of memories. This, too, finds its place in an ancillary poem, 'After All Soul's Day' ('the little, slender soul sits swiftly down, and takes the oars . . .').

Further on in the original draft, there is a whole area devoted to meditating about oblivion:

> row, little soul, row on,
> on the longest journey, towards the greatest goal.

> Neither straight nor crooked, neither here nor there
> but shadows folded on deeper shadows
> and deeper, to a core of sheer oblivion
> like the convolutions of shadow-shell
> or deeper, like the foldings and involvings of a womb.

> Drift on, drift on, my soul, towards the most pure
> most dark oblivion . . .

There is no direct equivalent for this, either, in the final version of 'The Ship of Death'; this idea of dissolving into oblivion. But in poems that seem ancillary the idea is developed in a dozen different ways. For instance:

[the soul] enters fold after fold of deepening darkness
for the cosmos even in death is like a dark whorled shell . . .

('Song of Death')

. . . But dipped, once dipped in dark oblivion
the soul has peace, inward and lovely peace.

('The End, The Beginning')

. . . Only in sheer oblivion are we with God . . . ('Forget')

And so on, also, in 'Sleep', 'Sleep and Waking' and 'Fatigue'. But this idea, so often reiterated in others among the *Last Poems* and deriving from the draft of 'The Ship of Death', is precisely what the final version of 'The Ship of Death' does not say. Take, for example, the image of the shell – 'convolutions of shadow-shell' in the draft, 'dark whorled shell' in 'Song of Death'. In the final version of 'The Ship of Death', the poem as we know it, the image is given, not to dissolution and oblivion, but to a vision of the soul in resurrection upon the far shore. The ship wings home: the spirit is made new. The word 'oblivion' occurs frequently in the draft, as it does in the ancillary poems, but it occurs in the draft as a divagation from the main theme. In the final poem the ship does not vanish, the soul does not disappear. On the contrary, the trunk of the poem is the marvellous idea, voiced in *Etruscan Places*, that the little bronze ship bears the soul not to dissolution but to a new life in the other world. Whatever diverges from this idea in the draft is cut out in revision and, as we have seen, is used for other poems. The beginning of 'The Ship of Death' is, it is true, virtually identical in draft and poem.

Now it is autumn and the falling fruit
and the long journey towards oblivion.

The apples falling like great drops of dew
to bruise themselves an exit from themselves . . .

But this is preliminary. It is the second strophe that brings in the central idea:

> Have you built your ship of death, O have you?
> O build your ship of death, for you will need it . . .

reinforced by, what we don't have in the draft, a rich autumnal imagery:

> The grim frost is at hand, when the apples will fall
> thick, almost thundrous, on the hardened earth.
> And death is on the air like a smell of ashes!
> Ah! can't you smell it?
>
> And in the bruised body, the frightened soul
> finds itself shrinking, wincing from the cold
> that blows upon it through the orifices . . .

There is no room in this structure for a meditation upon the souls crying upon the shore. That idea is relegated to the ancillary poems. Instead, Lawrence goes on to play imaginatively with the Shakespearian word, mentioned only in passing in the draft, 'quietus':

> And can a man his own quietus make
> with a bare bodkin?
>
> With daggers, bodkins, bullets, man can make
> a bruise or break of exit for his life;
> but is that a quietus, O tell me, is it quietus?
>
> Surely not so! for how could murder, even self-murder
> ever a quietus make . . .?

The word becomes further subdued, into 'quiet', and this provides the opportunity to restate explicitly, what has been implied throughout, the main theme:

> O let us talk of quiet that we know,
> that we can know, the deep and lovely quiet
> of a strong heart at peace!
>
> How can we this, our own quietus, make?
>
> Build then the ship of death, for you must take
> the longest journey, to oblivion . . .

The word 'oblivion' in this final version is used in a manner adjunctive to the concept of the ship – 'the long journey towards oblivion', 'the dark flight down oblivion', 'it is the end, it is oblivion'. The effect is that of a refrain; it never escalates, as it does in the draft, into a separate treatment of the concept 'oblivion'. It is held in check still, while the poem adumbrates the counter-theme – 'we are dying' – which in its turn merges with the positive: the building of the ship:

> We are dying, we are dying, so all we can do
> is now to be willing to die, and to build the ship
> of death to carry the soul on the longest journey . . .
> . . . Now launch the small ship, now as the body dies
> and life departs, launch out, the fragile soul
> in the fragile ship of courage, the ark of faith
> with its store of food and little cooking pans . . .

Here we have the preparation for that wonderful concept at the end, of the sea-worn soul emerging into its new life:

> The flood subsides, and the body, like a worn sea-shell
> emerges strange and lovely.
> And the little ship wings home, faltering and lapsing
> on the pink flood,
> and the frail soul steps out, into her house again
> filling the heart with peace.

The poems at the end of *Last Poems* may be ancillary to 'The Ship of Death', but that great work is not ancillary to those poems. It is a powerfully articulated structure. A poem such as 'Tortoises' succeeds cumulatively: it has many strokes at its theme and it comes across regardless of form, almost in spite of it. The same is true, on a smaller scale, of 'Snake'. But in 'The Ship of Death' the theme, form and emotion fuse into one. The one addendum that could be suggested is the fine poem 'Shadows'. This picks up the idea of oblivion, as the ancillary poems do, but, unlike them, applies it to the remaking of the soul.

> And if tonight my soul may find her peace
> in sleep, and sink in good oblivion,

> and in the morning wake like a new-opened flower
> then I have been dipped again in God, and new-created . . .

The effect, if one reads this poem immediately after 'The Ship of Death', is that of a rounding-off. It is thematically related yet structurally independent: a perfect coda.

'Bavarian Gentians', which I believe to be Lawrence's greatest poem, is in no need even of a coda. Lawrence here takes his place among the metaphysical poets of the twentieth century. The depth of the poem is astonishing: a sustained meditation welcoming what is, after all, our inevitable end. Here, even more than in 'The Ship of Death', Lawrence achieved union of theme and emotion with a structure capable of expressing them both: the magnificent concept of a dark flower, the gentian, as an inverse candle, guiding the soul's path down into the nether regions.

Like the tale, 'The Ladybird', it relates to the myth of Persephone, daughter of the fertility goddess Demeter, taken down to the Underworld by Pluto, its king. Here the myth works as a premonition of the peace of death, seen as a kind of dark glory:

> Not every man has gentians in his house
> in soft September, at slow, sad Michaelmas . . .

It is darkness visible: based on the optical fact that dark colours absorb light. There follows a rich and intense description of the flower. This, among other things, serves to associate its colour – partly through sonorities brought about by assonance – with the darkness of the King of the Ghosts:

> giving off darkness, blue darkness, as Demeter's pale
>   lamps give off light,
> lead me then, lead me the way . . .

Thus we are shown the purpose to which the gentians are to be put. Even after many readings of the poem, that quietly determined 'lead . . . lead . . .' may thrill the reader with recognition; for this is the *volta* of the poem, the turning-point. We now realize why the poet, unusually among men, has gentians in his house. He is marked out. The poem moves from quietly contemplating this symbol of the underworld to reaching it down as a torch.

From now on the lines spread out in weight and number of

syllables and, at the same time, move more slowly. This turning point is a slow and deliberate descent:

> Reach me a gentian, give me a torch!
> let me guide myself with the blue, forked torch of this flower
> down the darker and darker stairs, where blue is darkened
> on blueness
> even where Persephone goes, just now, from the frosted September
> to the sightless realm where darkness is awake upon
> the dark . . .

'Darkness is *awake* upon the dark' – through sound, idea and imagery Lawrence reveals below an inverted Pelion a profound Ossa. The language creates concept after concept of darkness, each one more intense than the last, until in the end we have entered an underworld far darker than the gloom of the slow, sad Michaelmas of the beginning. This is darker than the underworld in Milton, even: this is now darkness *in*visible. Persephone is enfolded in the gloom of Pluto – the passion of dense gloom – pierced with that passion. The verbs carry out a concept of dying; the nouns project darkness. And death is welcomed as marriage in the final apotheosis:

> among the splendour of torches of darkness, shedding
> darkness on the lost bride and her groom.

There is nothing better in the whole of Lawrence, prose or verse. This is a poem to be read alongside Donne's 'A Hymn to God my God, in my sickness', Herbert's 'Affliction', Vaughan's 'They are all gone into the world of light'.

But how are we to rank Lawrence as a poet? There are not many instances in English where a poet has had so few signal successes in proportion to his failures. In Pinto's edition of the Collected Poems there are 1037 titles. Of those, not more than perhaps forty-three can be recommended to the reader without considerable qualification. Lawrence's use of verse as a kind of emotional diary was not likely to result in many fully articulated structures. In this he resembles Cowper and Shelley, both of whom were capable of considerable heights but most of whose work is careless and poorly formed. But what happens if one compares the bulk of

Lawrence's work in verse with what he did in the form of the tale or of the story? One cannot help feeling that the poetry for the most part falls short of the certainty one expects to find in a great master. The earlier poems are fragments of perception, sketches, drafts. Even most of the later poems are triumphs not of technique but of occasion. It is a severe criterion to compare Lawrence not with his contemporaries but with himself. But such a comparison can only confirm one's feeling that Lawrence was at his best in his tales and stories. Even so, the poet Lawrence emerges as one of the few interesting contributors to the Imagist anthologies, the greatest of the Georgians and a redoubtable forerunner and contemporary of Thomas, Owen and Rosenberg. And in 'The Ship of Death' and 'Bavarian Gentians', as surely as in the best of his prose, Lawrence takes his place among the classics.

Appendix: Plays

Lawrence wrote ten plays. They must be considered as overflows from his central work. But they do have points of particular interest. *A Collier's Friday Night* (1906, 1909) is a conflation of several scenes which were to occur in *Sons and Lovers*; it seems to relate to an early draft of that book. Climactic to the play is a scene when the Lawrence-figure (Ernest) pays so much attention to the Miriam-figure (Maggie) that he burns the bread he should have been watching.

MOTHER   It's all very well, my son – you may talk about caring for me but when it comes to Maggie Pearson it's very little you care about me – or Nellie – or anybody else.

ERNEST   (*dashing his fingers through his hair*) You talk *just* like a woman! As if it makes any difference! As if it makes the least difference!

MOTHER   (*folding her hands in her lap and turning her face from him*) Yes, it does.

ERNEST   (*frowning fiercely*) It doesn't. Why should it? If I like apples, does it mean I don't like – bread? You know, Ma, it doesn't make any difference.

MOTHER   (*doggedly*) *I* know it does.

The Morel-figure, the old miner of the title, is finely achieved in speech whose vivacity of dialect shows what was to be Lawrence's especial forte in drama – 'It's a nice thing as a man as comes home from th' pit parched up canna ha'e a drink got 'im . . .' There is, in this dislocation of accepted syntax, a noticeable freedom from the conventional language of the drama of the time.

The Widowing of Mrs Holroyd (1910, 1913) relates to Lawrence's story 'Odour of Chrysanthemums'. The dramatic speech, as ever, is alive in its rhythms. Thus the wife, sponging the face of the dead miner: 'My dear, my dear – oh, my dear! I can't bear it, my dear – you shouldn't have done it. You shouldn't have done it. Oh – I can't bear it, for you. Why couldn't I do anything for you? The children's father – my dear – I wasn't good to you. But you shouldn't have done this to me . . .' Distantly, there is David's lament over Absalom in the Authorized Version; nearer home, the cadences of J. M. Synge in *Riders to the Sea*. It is no accident that Lawrence's gift for dialogue was praised by two great Irish playwrights, Bernard Shaw and Sean O'Casey.

Just as the first two plays relate to the early fiction, so *The Daughter-in-Law* (1913) foreshadows 'Fanny and Annie' which is a work of 1919. Here we see the life of the well-bred young woman after she has married an artisan; a miner, coddled by his over-bearing mother. In this case, the daughter-in-law does not find out about the impending child the miner has given to another woman until well after her marriage to him. The marriage has not so far been successful but this circumstance, together with the fact that the husband has been hurt while picketing a colliery-strike, brings the couple closer together, though uneasily so:

LUTHER   (*He sways as he takes his cap off*) Minnie –
MINNIE   My love – my love!
LUTHER   Minnie – I want thee ter ma'e what tha can o' me. (*He sounds almost sleepy.*)
MINNIE   (*crying*) My love – my love!
LUTHER   I know what tha says is true.
MINNIE   No, my love – it isn't – it isn't.
LUTHER   But if ter'lt ma'e what ter can o'me – an' then if ter has a childt – tha'lt happen ha'e enow.
MINNIE   No – no – it's you. It's you I want. It's you.

These three plays have obvious crudities – contrivances of entry and exit, jerks and disjunctions in plot. But their virtues in the linguistically exiguous twentieth-century theatre are rare indeed. They are written in a language which demands to be spoken and which turns vernacular into something very like dramatic poetry. And their concerns are the stuff of life: the social mores of what had been the submerged classes, the estrangement between

husband and wife, or, as here, their painful attempt at reconciliation.

The rest of Lawrence's dramatic output can be dealt with more
tersely. *The Merry-Go-Round* (1911) is a Derbyshire *As You Like
It* – rapid changes of partners, scenes of pantomime farce. *The
Married Man* (1912) retails the embarrassments of a local phil-
anderer who conceals from various willing ladies the fact that he
already has a wife and child. *The Fight for Barbara* (1912) shows
Lawrence in a very different vein – drawing upon his experience of
life with Frieda after their elopement. There are stirring scenes of
conflict between the guilty couple on the one hand and Barbara's
mother, father and deserted husband on the other. *Touch and Go*
(1918) shows Gerald Barlow, director of a colliery, contending
against a miners' strike. The play has a degree of interest as a
footnote to *Women in Love*, and the strike-leader bears more than
a fugitive relationship to the Aaron of *Aaron's Rod*.

Altitude (1924) is a sketch of the people surrounding Lawrence's
patroness, Mabel Dodge Luhan, in Taos: its interest is mainly biographical. *Noah's Flood* (1925) is the beginning of a morality play
in which the men of earth conspire together to overthrow the
power of Noah. And *David* (1925) is an ambitious historical
tragedy, based on the Biblical hero but giving considerable
extension to the role played by David's wife, Michal, and to the
stormily romantic figure made of Saul. But, unlike the early
realistic plays, the Biblical cadences of *David* are not mediated
through local speech and so lack colour and emphasis: 'I will wait
and watch till the day of David at last shall be finished, and wisdom
no more be fox-faced, and the blood gets back its flame. Yea, the
flame dies not, though the sun's red dies . . .'

As the follower of Synge and the contemporary of O'Casey,
Lawrence occupies no negligible place in the underpopulated
pantheon of modern dramatic masters. It is hard to think of
Lawrence as a playwright because his most achieved works in this
genre seem to be appendices to successes in his chosen area of
prose fiction. What one can say is that in a National Repertory, if
anything of the sort existed, there would be found a place for three
of Lawrence's plays: *A Collier's Friday Night, The Widowing of
Mrs Holroyd* and *The Daughter-in-Law*.

A Selective Bibliography

BIOGRAPHICAL

Aldington, Richard, *Portrait of a Genius, But* . . . (London, 1950)

Lawrence, D. H., *Letters*, Vols 1–7, ed. James T. Boulton and others (Cambridge, England, 1979–   )

Lawrence, Frieda, *The Memoirs and Correspondence* (including *Not I, But the Wind*), ed. E. W. Tedlock (London, 1961)

Moore, Harry T., *The Priest of Love* (New York and London, 1974)

Nehls, Edward, *D. H. Lawrence: A Composite Biography* (Madison, Wisconsin, 1957–9)

BIBLIOGRAPHICAL

Beebe, Maurice and Anthony Tommasi, 'Criticism of D. H. Lawrence: a Selected Checklist', *Modern Fiction Studies* V (1959)

D. H. Lawrence Review, ed. James C. Cowan and others, Vols 1– (Arkansas, 1968– ; contains valuable checklists of criticism of D. H. Lawrence comp. Richard D. Beards and others)

Draper, R. P., *D. H. Lawrence: The Critical Heritage* (London, 1970)

Roberts, Warren, *A Bibliography of D. H. Lawrence* (London, 1963)

Sagar, Keith and Lindeth Vasey, *D. H. Lawrence: A Calendar of his Works* (Manchester, 1979)

GENERAL CRITICISM

Cavitch, David, *Lawrence and the New World* (New York, 1969)

Cowan, James C., *D. H. Lawrence's American Journey* (Cleveland and London, 1970)

Daleski, H. M., *The Forked Flame* (Evanston, Illinois, and London, 1965)

Leavis, F. R., *D. H. Lawrence, Novelist* (London, 1955)

Leavis, F. R., *Thought, Words and Creativity* (London, 1976)
Moynahan, Julian, *The Deed of Life* (Princeton, N.J., and Oxford, 1963)
Sagar, Keith, *The Art of D. H. Lawrence* (Cambridge, England, 1966)
Worthen, John, *Lawrence and the Idea of the Novel* (London, 1979)

1 POEMS (1905–19)

Corke, Helen, 'D. H. Lawrence as I Saw Him', *Renaissance and Modern Studies* IV (1960)
Corke, Helen, *D. H. Lawrence: The Croydon Years* (Austin, Texas, 1965)
Farmer, David, '"The Turning Back": The Text and its Genesis', *D. H. Lawrence Review* V (1972)
Pound, Ezra, Review of *Love Poems* in *Poetry* II (1913; rep. Pound's *Selected Literary Criticism*, London, 1954) Another version rep. R. P. Draper, *D. H. Lawrence: The Critical Heritage* (London, 1970; see also in that vol. a review by Edward Thomas)
Tiedje, Egon, 'D. H. Lawrence's Early Poetry', *D. H. Lawrence Review* IV (1971; and see exchanges with Carole Ferrier, V, 1972 and also her article, 'D. H. Lawrence's Pre-1920 Poetry', VI, 1973)

2 STORIES (1907–19)

Cushman, Keith, *D. H. Lawrence at Work: The Emergence of the Prussian Officer Stories* (London and Virginia, 1978)
O'Connor, Frank, *The Lonely Voice* (London, 1964)
Sagar, Keith, Introduction, *The Mortal Coil and Other Stories* (Harmondsworth, 1971)

3 NOVELS (1906–13)

Chambers, Jessie ('E.T.'), *D. H. Lawrence: a Personal Record* (London, 1935)
Corke, Helen, 'Concerning *The White Peacock*', *Texas Quarterly* II (1959; rep. Corke, *D. H. Lawrence: The Croydon Years*, Austin, Texas, 1965)
Corke, Helen, 'The Writing of *The Trespasser*', *D. H. Lawrence Review* VII (1974)
Keith, W. J., 'D. H. Lawrence's *The White Peacock*', *University of Toronto Quarterly* XXXVII (1968)
Kuttner, Alfred Booth, '*Sons and Lovers*: A Freudian Appreciation',

Psychoanalytic Review III (1916; shorter version rep. R. P. Draper, *D. H. Lawrence: The Critical Heritage*, London, 1970)

Lawrence, Ada and Stuart Gelder, *Young Lorenzo* (Florence, 1931; London, 1932)

4 NOVELS (1913–16)

Cushman, Keith, ' "I am going through a transition stage": *The Prussian Officer* and *The Rainbow*', *D. H. Lawrence Review* VIII (1975)

Hobsbaum, Philip, *A Theory of Communication*, Chapter VI (London, 1970; published as *A Theory of Criticism* (Bloomington, Indiana, 1970)

Miko, Stephen J., *Towards Women in Love* (New Haven and London, 1972)

Robson, W. W., 'D. H. Lawrence and *Women in Love*', *The Modern Age*, Vol. VII, *Pelican Guide to English Literature*, ed. B. Ford (Harmondsworth, 1961)

Ross, Charles L., 'A Problem of Textual Transmission in the Typescripts of *Women in Love*', *The Library* XXIX (1974)

—— 'The Composition of *Women in Love*', *D. H. Lawrence Review* VIII (1975)

—— 'The Revision of the Second Generation in *The Rainbow*', *Review of English Studies* XXVII (1976)

—— 'D. H. Lawrence's Use of Greek Tragedy: Euripides and Ritual', *D. H. Lawrence Review* X (1977)

Stein, Walter, 'Criticism and Theology', *Life of the Spirit: a Blackfriars Review* (1964)

Worthen, John, 'Sanity, Madness and *Women in Love*', *Trivium* X (1975)

5 NOVELS (1913, 1920–28)

Atkinson, Curtis, 'Was There Fact in D. H. Lawrence's *Kangaroo*?' *Meanjin* XXIV (1965; and see also John Alexander, 'D. H. Lawrence's *Kangaroo*', in XXIV, 1965, preceding)

Clark, L. D., *The Dark Night of the Body* (Austin, Texas, 1964)

Lawrence, Ada and Stuart Gelder, *Young Lorenzo* (Florence, 1931; London, 1932)

Meyers, Jeffrey, '*The Plumed Serpent* and the Mexican Revolution', *Journal of Modern Literature* IV (1974)

Ober, William B., 'Lady Chatterley's *What?*' *Academy of Medicine of New Jersey Bulletin* XV (1969)

Rees, Marjorie, 'Mollie Skinner and D. H. Lawrence', *Westerly* I (1964)

6 TRAVEL, PHILOSOPHY, CRITICISM, PROPHECY

Hassall, Christopher, 'D. H. Lawrence and the Etruscans', *Essays by Divers Hands* XXI (1962)

Hinz, Evelyn J., 'The Beginning and the End: D. H. Lawrence's *Psychoanalysis* and *Fantasia*', *Dalhousie Review* LII (1972)

Leavis, F. R., 'The Wild, Untutored Phoenix', in *The Common Pursuit* (London, 1952)

Panichas, George, 'D. H. Lawrence and the Ancient Greeks', *English Miscellany* XVI (1965)

Weiner, S. Ronald, 'The Rhetoric of Travel: The Example of *Sea and Sardinia*', *D. H. Lawrence Review* II (1969; and see also David Ellis, X, 1977)

Williams, Raymond, *Culture and Society* (London, 1958)

7 TALES (1911, 1921–27)

Cowan, James C., 'D. H. Lawrence's Dualism: The Apollonian-Dionysian Polarity and "The Ladybird"', in *Forms of Modern British Fiction*, ed. A. W. Friedman (Austin, Texas, and London, 1975)

Dawson, Eugene W., 'Love Among the Mannikins: "The Captain's Doll"', *D. H. Lawrence Review* I (1968)

Ford, George H., *Double Measure* (New York, 1965)

Meyers, Jeffrey, 'The Voice of Water: "The Virgin and the Gipsy"', *English Miscellany* XXI (1970)

Powell, Laurence Clark, *Southwest Classics: The Creative Literature of the Arid Lands* (Pasadena, 1974)

Rossi, Patrizio, 'Lawrence's Two Foxes: A Comparison of the Texts', *Essays in Criticism* XXII (1972)

8 STORIES (1924–29)

Ross, Michael L., 'D. H. Lawrence's Second "Sun"', *D. H. Lawrence Review* VIII (1975; and see exchange in the same vol. with Brian Finney)

Sagar, Keith, Introduction to *The Princess and Other Stories* (Harmondsworth, 1971)

Willbern, David, 'Malice in Paradise: Isolation and Projection in "The Man Who Loved Islands"', *D. H. Lawrence Review* X (1977; and see Julian Moynahan on the subject in his *Deed of Life*, Princeton, N.J., and Oxford, 1963)

Zytaruk, George J., '"The Undying Man": D. H. Lawrence's Yiddish Story', *D. H. Lawrence Review* IV (1971)

9 POEMS (1920–29)

Lucie-Smith, Edward, 'The Poetry of D. H. Lawrence', in *D. H. Lawrence: Novelist, Poet, Prophet*, ed. S. Spender (New York and London, 1973)

Oates, Joyce Carol, *The Hostile Sun: The Poetry of D. H. Lawrence* (Los Angeles, 1973; rep. Oates, *New Heaven, New Earth* (New York, 1974)

Rich, Adrienne Cecile, 'Reflections on D. H. Lawrence's Poetry', *Poetry* CVI (1965)

Sagar, Keith, '"Little Living Myths": A Note on Lawrence's "Tortoises"', *D. H. Lawrence Review* III (1970)

APPENDIX: PLAYS

Sklar, Sylvia, *The Plays of D. H. Lawrence* (London, 1975)

Waterman, Arthur E., 'The Plays of D. H. Lawrence', *Modern Drama* II (1961)

Index

Works of D. H. Lawrence